BELMONT PARK

BELMONT PARK

THE CHAMPIONSHIP TRACK

KIMBERLY GATTO

Charleston London

THE
History
PRESS

Published by The History Press
Charleston, SC 29403
www.historypress.net

Front cover, top: Courtesy of Jason Moran. *Bottom*: Courtesy of Jessie Holmes.
Back cover, top: Courtesy of the Library of Congress. *Bottom*: Courtesy of Cindy Dulay, horse-races.net.

First published 2013

Manufactured in the United States

ISBN 978.1.60949.753.8

Library of Congress CIP data applied for.

Notice: The information in this book is true and complete to the best of our knowledge. It is offered without guarantee on the part of the author or The History Press. The author and The History Press disclaim all liability in connection with the use of this book.

For my mom,
Ann Gatto Urquhart,
for wholeheartedly supporting
my lifelong horse passion
and always believing in me
as a writer, horsewoman, daughter and friend.

K.A.G.

CONTENTS

CONTENTS

FOREWORD

Walking into Belmont Park for the first time some thirty-five years ago, I was much the same as a dewy-eyed freshman staring up at the ivy-covered walls on his first day at Harvard. Its rich history and intimidating size make the largest racetrack in America command respect. Yet, it's not the edifice but the stories that define the space.

Years later, as a reporter for the *Boston Globe*, I got to interview Hall of Fame trainer Woody Stephens, whose career is colorfully recalled by Kim Gatto in the marvelous history that follows. Woody had just published his memoir, *Guess I'm Lucky*, and it included engaging tales about his five consecutive Belmont Stakes victories. He introduced Diane, my wife, and me to several of his stakes winners, including Stephan's Odyssey and Belmont victor Crème Fraiche. As we sauntered through the shed row, Woody dispensed either a piece of carrot or a mint, whichever the horse preferred.

Later, we wandered through the backside with streets named after Man o' War and War Admiral before returning to his tiny office. Woody gave me a picture of himself standing beneath a street sign in Midway, Kentucky. He proudly pointed to the sign, which read, "W. Stephens St.," and boasted that he broke horses at Parrish Hill Farm just a few hundred yards from where a street was now named after him. "I guess I've come a long way," he said.

More than two decades later, Diane and I moved to Midway and lived on Mill Road Place, a street that runs off W. Stephens Street. On the eastern side of the main intersection, the street is named E. Stephens. I can still hear Woody laughing.

In 2002, my friend John Ciccolo and I drove from Boston to Belmont in the hopes of watching War Emblem follow up his victories in the Kentucky Derby and Preakness with a Belmont Stakes win and his coronation as the first Triple Crown winner since Affirmed. The crowd of more than 100,000 was the largest assemblage in Belmont Stakes history. A deafening roar arose as the classy three-year-olds moved into the gate, shaking the proud racetrack to the rafters. But War Emblem stumbled at the start and was only briefly competitive. The longest shot in Belmont Stakes history, Sarava, beat Medaglia d'Oro to the wire and paid $144.50. The hush at the finish seemed louder than the clamor at the start. It seems the only happy people were trainer Kenny McPeek and the owners, Mr. and Mrs. Gary Drake and Mr. and Mrs. Roy from England.

Ten years later, I ran into horseman and Midway mayor Tom Bozarth at the Grey Goose, a local bar and restaurant. He told me that he had a client who was trying to find a home for his retired stallion, which was currently residing in Florida. The client was Gary Drake. The horse was Sarava. A few weeks later, accompanied by generous checks from the Drakes and the Roys, Sarava arrived at Old Friends. The nearly black stallion resides in the front paddock, next to 1987 Belmont runner-up, Gulch.

In 2013, a few days before the Belmont Stakes, Sarava will be honored at a special party at Oheka Castle, just twenty minutes down the Long Island Expressway from Belmont Park. Gary Drake will be bringing his Belmont trophy, and jockey Edgar Prado will proudly recall his unexpected victory aboard this unlikely longshot.

As horse racing continues to confront declining attendance at racetracks across the country, Belmont Park is in danger of becoming the sport's equivalent of the SS *United States*, once the most impressive transatlantic ocean liner in history and now docked and decaying in Philadelphia. For those of us for whom racing is a sport with the greatest athletes in the world—Thoroughbreds and jockeys—it is so much more than speed figures and winning and losing tickets. It's the camaraderie and the color that can only be experienced through a day at the races. It's friends and beer and screaming and exultation and tossing tickets and cashing them and staring in wonder at the brilliance of the athletes. And there's no better place to spend a day at the races than at Belmont Park. May it endure forever.

MICHAEL BLOWEN

Founder and President
Old Friends
Georgetown, Kentucky

Acknowledgements

I would like to thank the following for their contributions to this book: Michael Blowen, the wonderful founder and president of Old Friends, for sharing his vast knowledge throughout the process; Allison Pareis, for providing excellent suggestions and photographs, as well as friendship; Jessie Holmes, Jason Moran, Cindy and Terence Dulay, Bud Morton, Adam and Bob Coglianese and the Keeneland Library for allowing me to use their wonderful photographs and for ensuring that I had all of the photographs that I needed; Pam Williams of the Belair Stable Museum for providing photographs and valuable support along the way; Vivien Morris, Louise Martin and Tim Ford for providing feedback and support; Patrick Lennon and my brother, Michael Gatto, for their excellent edits of the manuscript; Whitney Landis, Julia Turner and Dani McGrath of The History Press for their support throughout the project; and my family members and friends (and, of course, my horses) for their continued love and support.

Chapter 1

A RACECOURSE IN THE CITY

Thoroughbred horse racing in New York has a rich and storied history. The state's first formal racecourse was established in the 1600s, shortly after the arrival of British settlers in the new colony. At the request of England's King Charles II, colonial governor Richard Nicolls constructed a racetrack on the Salisbury Plains, located on what is now the Hempstead Plains on Long Island. Charles, a passionate fan of—and participant in—the sport, was insistent that horse racing be enjoyed in the new colony. The new racecourse, named Newmarket in honor of Charles's home track in England, was situated just a few miles away from what is now Belmont Park.

The next 150 years witnessed the development of various small area racecourses. These tracks, established by affluent landowners, were used for sport rather than as business ventures. As races were often paired with "unsavory" activities such as gambling, New York State placed a ban on horse racing in 1802. This ban lasted until 1819 and was reestablished the following year before being lifted in 1821 for the Queens County area. Following the removal of the ban, a new track called Union Course was constructed in Woodhaven, Queens County. The *New York Times* proclaimed Union Course to be "the racing centre for the territory around New York," noting that it was "so well laid out that it was used as the model for many of the big running and trotting tracks in other parts of the country." Union Course was the first racetrack to offer a "skinned," or dirt, surface, as races had previously been run on grass or "turf."

In the years that followed, Union Course showcased some of the greatest racehorses of the era, frequently in match races that pitted one animal against another. While the course did not include a grandstand, spectators flocked in hordes to the track, viewing the races in close quarters from both sides of the road; some, wanting a better vantage point, watched from atop nearby trees. British traveler William Blane noted in his journals that horse racing at this time "roused more interest than a presidential election."[1]

In 1825, a course for trotting horses, Centreville, was built in Queens County. By this time, horse racing had made its way through other areas of New York, albeit in a less organized manner. Riders often raced one another through busy city streets, creating a hazard for pedestrians and carriage drivers alike. Despite being forbidden by city officials, these informal races continued to occur for quite some time.

In addition to such informal "street races," organized racing continued to prosper in the early part of the nineteenth century. By 1836, there were nearly 130 meets for Thoroughbreds throughout the United States, and sales of such horses averaged $500,000 annually. Interest in the sport continued to rise in New York's high society; attending the races became one of the most fashionable activities of the era. The popularity of racing skyrocketed in 1863 with the establishment of the Saratoga Race Course in bucolic Saratoga Springs.

Founded by former prizefighter John Morrissey, "the Spa" at Saratoga quickly became the summer playground for the rich and famous. For several weeks in July and August, the racecourse hosted a dazzling array of politicians, royalty and big-spending jet setters. Lucrative purses attracted the nation's best Thoroughbreds, which galloped their way to fame and fortune at the "August place to be." Saratoga's "midsummer Derby," the Travers Stakes, became the highlight of the East Coast's summer racing season.

As the Civil War raged through the states, horse racing gained in popularity, particularly at Saratoga. Wealthy socialites traveled to the racecourse to drink its storied mineral waters, bet on the races and socialize in John Morrissey's opulent clubhouse. Patrons whittled their days away at the racetrack before moving to the nearby casino for the evening activities. The war did little to distract would-be gamblers from visiting Saratoga, as its carnival-like atmosphere offered a temporary escape from the troubles plaguing the nation. However, while racing continued to thrive after the war in the pastoral setting of Saratoga, the sport had become virtually nonexistent in New York City.

The absence of racing within city limits caught the attention of financier Leonard Jerome, who had assisted John Morrissey in the establishment of the Saratoga Race Course. Jerome was a successful businessman who maintained interests in several railroad companies and newspapers. Arguably one of the wealthiest men in New York, he was known to many as "the King of Wall Street." Jerome was also the founder of the Academy of Music, one of the first opera houses in New York City.

In addition to business and the arts, Jerome had a keen interest in horse racing. He was highly active as both a horse owner and an administrator and was, in fact, one of the original founders of the American Jockey Club. According to sources, Jerome was a devoted horse owner who spared no expense when it came to his animals and barns. The website *Daytonian in Manhattan* noted:

> *The stables, separated from the house by a small lot, were built to match the mansion, including stained glass windows—extremely ritzy accommodations for Jerome's horses. In a somewhat unusual arrangement, the ballroom was originally installed in the second floor of the stables.*[2]

As both a New York resident and a key player in the racing industry, Jerome recognized a need for a track that would cater to the needs of urban dwellers. Many of New York's businessmen were horse owners, like Jerome, and a racetrack in the city would be convenient for them. Additionally, residents from lower social classes would undoubtedly enjoy

Harper's Weekly lithograph of Jerome Park. *Library of Congress photo.*

attending the races, whether for occasional betting or a family outing. The expense of traveling to Saratoga Springs was cost prohibitive for everyday folks, who would enjoy watching the thrill of live horses in action. Leonard Jerome decided to capitalize on this market with the establishment of Jerome Park.

In 1866, Jerome purchased the estate of James Bathgate near Old Fordham Village in Westchester County (in what is now the Bronx). The mansion would serve as the summer home for the Jerome family while the sprawling grounds, measuring 230 acres, would provide ample land for the new racecourse. The location was easily accessible by carriage or railcar, enabling owners to readily transport their prized Thoroughbreds to the track.

To further simplify travel to the track, Jerome and his brother Lawrence established a wide boulevard stretching from Macombs Dam across the Harlem River to the racecourse. According to sources, New York authorities later attempted to name this stretch Murphy Avenue as a tribute to a local politician, but it is alleged that Jerome's wife installed a series of bronze plaques along the perimeters of the road that boldly decreed the name of the road as Jerome Avenue. In time, city officials relented, and the street became formally known by that name.

While both the road and racetrack were named in honor of Leonard Jerome, he cannot be solely credited for the development of Jerome Park. For that task, he enlisted the assistance of his friend August Belmont I, who shared Jerome's passions for both horse racing and the arts. In fact, Belmont and his wife frequented Jerome's opera houses, and Belmont himself had served as president of the Academy of Music.

Belmont, like Jerome, saw the need for a racetrack within city limits. The two men realized that in order

August Belmont I. *Library of Congress photo.*

for the venture to be profitable, the support of wealthy patrons was essential. To that end, they established a luxurious clubhouse that would accommodate thousands of spectators in style. The building was constructed on a rise, known as "the Bluff," which offered an all-encompassing view of the track and its grounds. The property was surrounded by an attractive picket fence, adding to its old-world charm. The *New York Times* later described Jerome Park as "one of the most charming spots in America that has ever been devoted to the interest of sport."[3]

Jerome Park's opening on September 25, 1866, marked the formal return of Thoroughbred racing to the New York City area. More than twenty thousand spectators were in attendance for opening day, among them the Civil War hero (and later U.S. president) General Ulysses S. Grant. The *New York Daily Tribune* wrote:

> *Country folk and portly citizens have all turned out in their most gorgeous raiment* [clothing] *to witness the beginning of a new Olympiad in the art of horse breaking. On the ridge at the base of the yon heavily wooded fringe are grouped in thick masses at least 20,000 people of different classes and castes in the social estate, all eager and showing every tension to get a glance of the heroic quadrupeds who have made fame synonymous with their names in the history of the American Turf.*
>
> *Outside the picket fences surrounding the enclosure there are thousands of spectators congregated, who have not the dollar to pay the admission fee, and are compelled, therefore, to elongate their necks to distinguish the horses about to run. The rules declare that no liquor shall be sold on the ground, but enterprising tradesmen and hucksters pitch their tents as near the enclosure as they dare, and entice the thirsty souls from the excitements of the race.*[4]

Despite its popularity, Jerome Park's reign was to be short lived. It would be closed a mere twenty-four years later, as the land was needed to create a reservoir for the New York City water supply system. Nevertheless, during its heyday, Jerome Park contributed significantly to New York history. Some sources allege that Leonard Jerome's daughter Jennie met her future husband, Lord Randolph Churchill, at the racetrack; their union would, years later, produce Sir Winston Churchill. Additionally, the park served as the site of the first outdoor polo match.

By most accounts, however, it was in horse racing that Jerome Park left its greatest legacy. The track introduced several key races that have become woven into the fabric of U.S. racing history. These include the Champagne

Stakes for juveniles, modeled after the British race of the same name, and the Jerome Stakes, the second-oldest stakes race in the nation. Another event inaugurated at Jerome Park, the Ladies' Handicap, was the earliest U.S. stakes race for fillies and mares. And perhaps most importantly, in 1867, Jerome Park hosted the first-ever Belmont Stakes.

Chapter 2

THE PATRIARCH

Long before the establishment of the Belmont Stakes, its namesake was born worlds away, in Alzey, Prussia. August Belmont I (born August Schonberg) was a strong and colorful character with dark, piercing eyes and long sideburns that extended to the crest of his chin. Belmont entered the world on December 8, 1813, the first child born to Simon Schonberg and his wife, Frederika. Simon Schonberg was a prominent Jewish businessman and an active member of the local temple.

Tragedy struck the young Schonberg family in June 1921, when Frederika died shortly after delivering the couple's third child. Simon, unable to solely care for his children, sent the school-aged August to Frankfurt, Germany, where the boy could be raised by relatives. The boy's German grandmother, Gertrude, was connected by marriage to the Rothschilds, several brothers who maintained a vast empire in London, Paris and Vienna. As a testament to its prominence, the Rothschild family was awarded its own coat of arms by the emperor of Austria.

August Schonberg was well educated from an early age, counting Latin, Hebrew and several other languages among his fields of study. The boy longed to learn the English language as well, but for reasons unknown, his father would not allow it. One of the Rothschild brothers, Baron Carl von Rothschild, stepped in at this time, arranging for English and mathematics lessons for the boy. In response, Simon Schonberg refused to pay his son's tuition.

In an effort to subsidize his own education, young August obtained a job with the Rothschilds. The boy's duties consisted primarily of sweeping

August Belmont I. *Library of Congress photo.*

floors, polishing woodwork and running various errands for the brothers. August's maturity and strong work ethic impressed the Rothschilds, who frequently entrusted him with additional tasks. After completing his work-study in 1832, he was rapidly promoted, first to confidential clerk and later to private secretary, a position that required various travel assignments. As he spent time in Naples, Rome and Paris, August became well versed in the world of international finance. With his sights set on a career in business, the young man exchanged the ethnic-sounding Schonberg (which translates to "beautiful mountain") for its more aristocratic-sounding French translation, Belmont.

Armed with a new surname and keen business savvy, August Belmont boarded a ship bound for Havana in May 1837 to investigate the Rothschilds' Cuban interests. While on a layover in New York, Belmont discovered that hundreds of local businesses and financial institutions were about to crash. An ardent businessman, Belmont realized that he could capitalize on the soon-to-be defunct businesses before word of their demise had spread through the ranks. He quickly purchased several companies and parcels of real estate on credit terms, at prices well below their pre-crash value. Belmont replaced the Rothschilds' defunct American Agency with his own August Belmont & Co. and established an office at 78 Wall Street in New York City. Backed by the Rothschilds' reputation and Belmont's own business sense, the new company flourished.

August Belmont's life among the well-heeled Rothschilds had fostered in him a sense of culture and nobility. Buoyed by his business income, Belmont purchased one of the first mansions for sale on New York's newly fashionable Fifth Avenue at Fourteenth Street. In the evenings he socialized among the elite at various parties and balls. At one such event, Belmont was introduced to Caroline Slidell Perry, daughter of Commodore Matthew Perry of the U.S. Navy. Belmont was smitten with the lovely young woman and, after an appropriate courtship, asked for her hand in marriage. It is alleged, however, that there was at least some hesitation from Commodore Perry, who became concerned when questions surfaced regarding Belmont's past. Years earlier, false rumors had surfaced that Belmont—a German Jew—was in fact an illegitimate son of the Rothschilds. Writers for the *New York Herald*, reportedly jealous of Belmont's financial and social standing, had perpetuated these rumors, resulting in the young man's involvement in at least one altercation.

Rumors aside, Commodore Perry ultimately gave his blessing to the young couple. August Belmont and Caroline Perry were thus married on November 7, 1849, in New York's Church of the Ascension. The nuptials had been postponed from October 31—not as a result of any objection from the commodore but rather because Belmont's birth certificate had not yet arrived from overseas. Prior to the wedding, Belmont converted from Judaism to his wife's Episcopal faith. The young family expanded quickly, welcoming a son, Perry, in 1850. Another son, August Jr., was born in February 1853, followed by daughters Frederika in 1854 and Jane Pauline ("Jeannie") in 1856.

Caroline Perry Belmont hailed from an established family that maintained an active involvement in politics. Her uncle John Slidell was a well-known U.S. representative and senator. Slidell took an interest in August Belmont, encouraging him to campaign in New York for candidate James Buchanan. Belmont agreed, writing letters to various publications endorsing Buchanan as a candidate. Despite Belmont's best efforts, however, Buchanan lost out to Franklin Pierce, who ultimately won the nomination of the Democratic Party. Belmont subsequently became a staunch supporter of Pierce and endured undue criticism of his Jewish heritage by Pierce's opponents.

In 1853, Pierce appointed August Belmont as chargé d'affaires and minister to The Hague, the capital city of the province of South Holland in the Netherlands. During this appointment, Belmont became involved in the assembly of the Ostend Manifesto, a document that recommended that the United States purchase Cuba from Spain, implying that the United States should declare war if Spain refused the sale. This involvement likely cost Belmont the position as ambassador to Spain in 1856. Therefore, after the end of his term at The Hague in 1858, Belmont and his family returned to the United States. That same year, the family welcomed son Oliver Hazard Perry Belmont; another son, Raymond, would be born three years later.

Belmont's support for the Democratic Party continued over the next several years, and in 1860, he backed Senator Stephen A. Douglas as the Democratic candidate. Douglas's position on slavery resulted in a split in the party, ultimately handing the victory to Republican Abraham Lincoln. Following President Lincoln's election and the onset of the Civil War, Belmont assisted the United States by lending gold to the government in order to help finance the war efforts. However, Belmont's Jewish background remained a source of criticism from the media.

Belmont eventually put politics aside and turned toward the business of horse racing.

Chapter 3

THE TEST OF THE CHAMPION

O wing perhaps to the influence of his friend Leonard Jerome, August Belmont developed a strong passion for equestrian sports. This interest likely began as a fondness for carriage driving and later extended to Thoroughbred racing. By 1867, Belmont was an active participant in the sport; he served as the first president of the American Jockey Club, which oversaw all New York racing at that time. That same year, he established Nursery Stud, a breeding facility based on 1,100 acres in Babylon, New York. Belmont purchased the bay stallion Kentucky, the winner of the inaugural Travers Stakes, as a foundation stallion for his operation.

Kentucky, sired by the legendary Lexington, was one of the greatest racers of his era. The lanky bay was the undisputed champion of the East Coast, winning a string of twenty consecutive races, including the first running of the Travers Stakes at Saratoga in 1864. The colt was skilled at distances from two to four miles; when he galloped to victory in the Inaugural Stakes at Jerome Park that same year, the race was run in grueling four-mile heats. Kentucky had been purchased for the hefty sum of $40,000 by Leonard Jerome, who subsequently sold him to Annieswood Stable, a partnership in which Belmont was a member. Belmont ultimately purchased the colt for $15,000 and sent him to stand at Nursery Stud; his offspring would include the champion filly Woodbine.

As a breeder of Thoroughbreds, Belmont believed that soundness and stamina were the building blocks for success in racing. Belmont, like many of his contemporaries, studied the bloodlines of British horses that won distance races such as the Epsom Derby and the St. Leger Stakes. These horses were bred for endurance and were able to tackle a course well over a mile in length while still

Edward Troye portrait of the stallion Kentucky. *Library of Congress photo.*

retaining an extra "kick" at the finish line. Such horses would be able to increase their speed in the final stretch, when the early leaders typically faded.

It was this desire for stamina that led Belmont to create a new race. The aptly named Belmont Stakes, inaugurated in 1867, would originally be run at a distance of one mile and five-eighths, similar to the great races in Europe. The Belmont is the fourth-oldest stakes race in North America, predated only by the Phoenix Stakes at Keeneland (first run in 1831), the Queen's Plate in Canada (1860) and the Travers at Saratoga Race Course (1864). Additionally, the Belmont Stakes was the first of the eventual "Triple Crown" races in the United States, predating both the Preakness Stakes (1873) and the Kentucky Derby (1875). Due to its challenging distance, the Belmont Stakes would later be referred to as the "test of the champion."

DISTANCE OF THE BELMONT STAKES	
Years	**Distance**
1867–1873	One and five-eighths miles
1874–1889	One and one-half miles
1890, 1891, 1892, 1895, 1904, 1905	One and one-quarter miles
1893 and 1894	One and one-eighth miles
1896–1903 and 1906–1925	One and three-eighths miles
1926–present	One and one-half miles

The inaugural Belmont Stakes took place at Jerome Park on Thursday, June 19, 1867. The race offered a lucrative purse of $1,500 added to a total purse of $2,500. The winner's share was $1,850, which translates to a modern-day purse of $31,000. While the race originally reported eleven entries, seven dropped out prior to post time, allegedly in fear of a speedy colt named Monday, which was owned by New Yorker Francis Morris.

The race began as expected, with Monday sent off as the odds-on favorite. According to sources, Morris was confident that his colt would be victorious, based on a plan that he had developed with his jockey. Prior to post time, Morris gave the jockey explicit instructions to hold Monday back, allowing the early leaders to set the pace and ultimately tire out. However, a colt named De Courcey caught both Morris and the jockey off guard, as the horse set blazing early fractions with no signs of slowing down.

Jockey Gilbert Patrick, known to racegoers as "Gilpatrick," was aboard Morris's other entry, the bay filly Ruthless. Gilpatrick, a quick thinker, realized that Morris's strategy for Monday was not going as planned. Nudging the filly toward the lead, Gilpatrick attempted to slow the leader

Edward Troye portrait of Ruthless, winner of the first Belmont Stakes. *Library of Congress photo.*

down by entering into a speed duel. His plan was to tire De Courcey out, making way for Monday to gain the lead. However, the typically swift-footed Monday flattened out, ultimately finishing in last place.

Over a track that was deemed "heavy," Ruthless bested De Courcey by a neck to win the inaugural Belmont Stakes. The *New York Times* described the effort as a "splendid race home" and "a most exciting finish."[5] In a time of three minutes and five seconds, Ruthless secured herself a place in racing history.

Despite his disappointment with Monday's poor performance, Morris happily accepted the inaugural winner's trophy. For her part, Ruthless proved that the win was no fluke; she went on to win the 1867 Travers Stakes at Saratoga, carrying 103 pounds over a course of a mile and three-quarters. The game filly completed her racing career with a record of seven wins and four places in eleven starts and is widely recognized as one of the greatest female racers of her time.

Following the victory of Ruthless, the Belmont Stakes became a showcase for the greatest Thoroughbreds and attracted the sport's most successful owners. August Belmont I often entered his own horses in the race. In 1869, he dominated the winner's purse when his Fenian and Glenelg placed first and second, respectively. In addition to breeding and racing his own stable, Belmont remained a key player in the New York racing establishment for many years. In 1870, he assisted in the development of Monmouth Park in Oceanport, New Jersey.

The 1870 Belmont Stakes was won by the colt Kingfisher, another son of the famous stallion Lexington. A lanky bay with a narrow blaze, Kingfisher was purchased in 1868 by Daniel Swigert for the sum of $490. Swigert, a former manager at Woodburn Stud in Kentucky, enjoyed great success with the colt under the watchful eye of trainer Rollie Colston. In addition to the Belmont Stakes, Kingfisher won the 1870 Travers Stakes at Saratoga, as well as the Champion Stakes and the Annual Stakes. Following these victories, Swigert sold the colt to August Belmont I for a reported sum of $15,000. Unfortunately, the horse was sidelined by an injury at Saratoga in 1871 and never returned to his previous level of greatness on the track. He did, however, sire seven stakes winners. Among Kingfisher's offspring were Lady Rosebery, winner of the 1880 Champagne Stakes, and Prince Royal, who captured the 1888 Jerome Handicap.

A year after Kingfisher's victory, another son of Lexington galloped to victory in the Belmont Stakes. Harry Bassett, a chestnut colt, won the race by three lengths over Stockwood in a time of two minutes, fifty-six seconds, carrying 110 pounds. August Belmont collected a portion of the 1871 winnings as his entry, By The Sea, finished third. The winner's purse was $5,400, which translates to

Kingfisher, winner of the 1870 Belmont Stakes. *Library of Congress photo.*

1871 Belmont Stakes winner Harry Bassett. *Library of Congress photo.*

Springbok, winner of the 1873 Belmont Stakes. *Library of Congress photo.*

approximately $105,000 as of 2013. For his part, Harry Bassett would be undefeated in nine consecutive starts that season, with key wins including the Jerome Handicap and the Travers Stakes. The horse was trained by David McDaniel, who also happened to own the animal.

Harry Bassett's Belmont victory was no fluke for McDaniel; the owner and trainer would win the next two runnings of the Belmont Stakes with Joe Daniels and Springbok, respectively. Both of these horses were ridden by a young jockey by the name of James G. Rowe Sr. Born in Virginia, Rowe had been working in the racing industry since his boyhood; by age fourteen, he had become the leading jockey in the nation. Struggling to maintain weight, Rowe would switch from riding to training at the age of eighteen, earning great fame in this role. In 1881, he became the youngest trainer to win the Kentucky Derby with the victory of the colt Hindoo, and in 1915, he trained Regret, the first filly to win the Derby. Amid these honors, Rowe enjoyed perhaps his greatest success in the Belmont Stakes. Between 1883 and 1913, he would amass eight Belmont Stakes victories—more than any other trainer as of this writing. Rowe's son, James Jr., would also become a successful trainer, guiding the colt Twenty Grand to victory in the 1931 Kentucky Derby and Belmont Stakes.

As an aside, it is unknown whether any of the aforementioned equine champions donned the garland of white carnations that has become tradition in the Belmont Stakes winner's circle. The exact origin of this custom remains shrouded in mystery. Regardless of its earliest appearance, the white carnation is an appropriate choice to adorn the Belmont Stakes winner. The flower is known for its hardiness and strength, befitting the winner of the "test of the champion."

Chapter 4

MORRIS PARK AND THE END OF AN ERA

Throughout the 1870s, the Belmont Stakes continued to attract the greatest horses to Jerome Park. In 1874, the race crowned its first foreign-bred winner, the brown colt Saxon. The horse was foaled in England and imported to the United States by businessman Pierre Lorillard, who would later earn fame as the owner of the champion colt Parole. Saxon won the Belmont in exhilarating fashion, passing Grinstead by a mere neck at the end of one and a half miles at a time of two minutes and thirty-nine and a half seconds.

FOREIGN-BORN WINNERS OF THE BELMONT STAKES		
Year	**Horse**	**Country**
1874	Saxon	Great Britain
1898	Bowling Brook	Great Britain
1917	Hourless	Great Britain
1918	Johren	Great Britain
1957	Gallant Man	Great Britain
1958	Cavan	Ireland
1960	Celtic Ash	Great Britain
1990	Go and Go	Ireland
1998	Victory Gallop	Canada

Spendthrift, winner of the 1879 Belmont Stakes. *Library of Congress photo.*

In 1879, the colt Spendthrift became the first of owner James R. Keene's horses to capture the Belmont Stakes. In the years to come, Keene, a prominent Wall Street stockbroker, would amass a whopping six victories in the "test of the champion." This record would be matched in the mid-1900s by William Woodward's legendary Belair Stud and, as of this writing, has yet to be surpassed.

Spendthrift, a dark chestnut with a star and two hind socks, was foaled at Woodburn Stud and purchased for the sum of $1,000 by Daniel Swigert. According to author E.S. Montgomery in *The Thoroughbred*, Swigert named the colt after his wife's propensity for luxurious spending in New York. The colt raced, undefeated, as a two-year-old for Swigert and was subsequently sold to Keene for the sum of $15,000. In addition to winning the Belmont Stakes, Spendthrift cruised to victory in the Lorillard Stakes and the Jersey Derby. At the age of five, he was retired to stud duty; his offspring would include Hastings, winner of the 1896 Belmont Stakes.

As the years passed, new traditions were introduced and records were set at Belmont Park. The year 1880 marked the first post parade at the Belmont Stakes; prior to that, horses were led directly from the paddock to the starting area. That year, the race was won by Grenada, the second of

Hanover, winner of the 1887 Belmont Stakes. *Library of Congress photo.*

three Belmont Stakes winners owned by Pierre Lorillard's brother, George. A tobacco manufacturer by trade, George Lorillard would also capture the Belmont trophy with Duke of Magenta (1878) and Saunterer (1881). George Lorillard would later be instrumental in the development of Monmouth Park Racetrack in New Jersey.

In 1887, the chestnut colt Hanover dominated the Belmont Stakes, romping to a fifteen-length victory over his only competitor, Oneko. Hanover, a son of the great Hindoo, won twenty of twenty-seven races that year at distances from four furlongs to two miles. As a stud, Hanover became the first American stallion to top the Leading Sire in North America list for four consecutive years; this record would not be duplicated for another seventy-eight years.

As records continued to be set in the Belmont Stakes, its namesake, August Belmont, was an active participant in the sport. Owing to his age and failing health, Belmont ceased campaigning his horses in 1882 but would remain a key player in the industry until the latter part of the decade. As his health would allow, he oversaw the operations of Nursery Stud, importing the stallion St. Blaise, winner of the 1883 Epsom Derby, to the United States at the end of the 1884 racing season.

In November 1890, Belmont passed away at his home in New York and was buried in Newport, Rhode Island, leaving an estate estimated at more than $10 million. That same year, *The Letters, Speeches and Addresses of August Belmont* was published in New York. Following Belmont's death, several of the Nursery Stud horses were sold at auction, including St. Blaise, which was sold to Tennessean Charles Reed for the lofty price of $100,000. The horse was subsequently sold to James Ben Ali Haggin, owner of Kentucky Derby winner Ben Ali. St. Blaise would return to Nursery Stud in later years after being purchased back by the Belmont family but would die tragically in a barn fire in 1909.

Prior to August Belmont I's passing, the Belmont Stakes had been moved to Morris Park in the Bronx. The relocation was born of necessity, as the land occupied by Jerome Park was used to build a reservoir for the city. With the impending closure of Jerome Park, businessman John Albert Morris established the new racetrack, appointing Leonard Jerome as its inaugural president. Morris Park was described by the *New York Times* as "the finest race track in the world," boasting a huge grandstand and a one-and-three-eighths-mile track that included various inclines. The stables at Morris Park could easily accommodate one thousand horses, more than any two of the other American racetracks combined at that time. Additionally, Morris Park's location provided easy access to New York City not only via horse and carriage but also by way of the New York, New Haven and Hartford Railroad.

In 1890, Morris Park hosted both the Preakness and the Belmont Stakes, which were held on the same day, June 10. This was due to a shift in the industry, which resulted in the Preakness being moved from its home base at Pimlico Race Course in Maryland. The Preakness would not be run again until 1894, when it was held at Gravesend Race Track on Coney Island in New York. In 1909, it would return to Pimlico, where it would eventually become known as the second jewel in the Triple Crown of Thoroughbred racing.

While the Preakness was moving from place to place, the Belmont Stakes was held solely at Morris Park from 1890 through 1904. The race card at Morris Park during this period also included the Champagne Stakes and the Ladies' Handicap, formerly held at Jerome Park. Additionally, Morris Park hosted the inaugural Metropolitan Handicap (later known as the "Met Mile") and the Matron Stakes in 1891 and 1892, respectively.

Before his death in 1895, John Morris had leased the race course to the Westchester Racing Association, which had been founded by Belmont's son, August Jr. Several renovations were made during this period, most notably a modification of the track from one and one-half miles to one mile to enable better viewing by spectators. However, attendance at the races was low, particularly by members of high society who had frequented Jerome Park in its heyday. In 1902, as attendance continued to plummet and the association battled difficulties with the lease, the decision was made to exit Morris Park and find an alternate site for the Belmont Stakes and other marquis races. The final day of horse racing was held on October 15, 1904.

Prior to the cessation of horse racing at Morris Park, the *Illustrated Sporting News* wrote:

> *No course in the country has ever enjoyed a greater popularity than the one at Morris Park, conducted by the Westchester Racing Association. When, therefore, it was announced last year that the property was to be devoted to other uses, those who for years had enjoyed the pleasures of attending entertainments at this picturesque spot were filled with apprehension…But hardly had the ink become dry on the printed articles announcing the retirement of Morris Park from the scenes of racing activity, before the supremacy of the Westchester Racing Association asserted itself.*[6]

To many, the closure of yet another racetrack may have pointed to somber days for Thoroughbred racing. Yet the end of horse racing at Morris Park was merely a bend in the road toward greater things to come. While August Belmont had left a lasting impact on the sport, his son, August Jr., had even grander prospects in mind. Unbeknownst to the racing public, Belmont was about to change the history of the sport.

Chapter 5

THE BIRTH OF "BIG SANDY"

Augthe Belmont Jr. was a horseman through and through. Whatever passion for horses his father had possessed, the younger Belmont had in spades. An athletic young man, Belmont Jr. was an avid polo player and, in fact, had participated in one of the first organized matches in the nation. Aside from his equestrian pursuits, the younger Belmont was an accomplished sprint runner. While a student at Harvard University, he introduced the use of spiked track shoes to the United States.

After graduating from Harvard in 1875, Belmont Jr. started a successful career in business. He began work at his father's banking house, where he would one day rise to the position of director. Perhaps more notably, Belmont Jr. founded the Interborough Rapid Transit Company, which built and operated the original underground New York City Subway line in 1902. To add to his list of accomplishments, Belmont was instrumental in the construction of the Cape Cod Canal, an artificial waterway that connects Cape Cod to the rest of Massachusetts.

Despite such achievements, many believe it was in horse racing that Belmont Jr. realized his greatest triumph. In 1894, he was one of the founding members of the Jockey Club, which maintains the studbook for all North American Thoroughbreds. He was a highly successful breeder both of polo ponies and Thoroughbreds, having inherited his father's Nursery Stud with operations in New York and Kentucky.

In addition to his American interests, Belmont Jr. maintained horse racing and breeding operations overseas. In 1908, his American-bred colt Norman

Portrait of August Belmont Jr. *Library of Congress photo.*

August Belmont Jr. at the races. *Library of Congress photo.*

III won the 2,000 Guineas, one of England's classic races. That same year, Belmont established Haras de Villers, a farm in Upper Normandy, France, where he bred champions such as Vulcain and Qu'elle est Belle. In later years, when racing in New York State was temporarily banned, Belmont would stand some of his American stallions at Haras de Villers.

Under Belmont Jr., Nursery Stud would produce an astounding 129 stakes champions, including the champion filly Beldame and 3 winners of the Belmont Stakes, most notably the great Man o' War. The first homebred Belmont Stakes victor, in 1902, was Masterman, a son of the talented but temperamental Hastings. The latter, which had won the 1896 running of the Belmont, was noted for his difficult nature. Allegedly, Hastings's handlers armed themselves with large sticks in his presence, as he had attempted to attack a stablehand on at least one occasion.

Bred in Kentucky by Dr. D.J. Neet, Hastings was sired by Spendthrift out of the mare Cinderella. Reportedly ill-tempered, Cinderella was a good producer; her offspring also included Kentucky Derby winner

Plaudit. As a yearling, Hastings was purchased for $2,800 by John Daly and David Gideon, for whom he won several juvenile races before the partnership was disbanded. The colt was later purchased by August Belmont Jr. for $37,000, a record sum for a young Thoroughbred at that time in history.

The purchase was well worth its price for Belmont, as the horse won the Tobaggan Handicap in 1896 and capped it off with a win in the Belmont Stakes. He was known to carry weights of up to 140 pounds with ease and also defeated older horses. Hastings's success was magnified in the breeding shed, as his offspring included William Collins Whitney's filly Gunfire, winner of the Metropolitan Handicap, and the aforementioned Belmont Stakes winner Masterman. Hastings's most famous offspring, however, was the chestnut colt Fair Play, sire of the legendary Man o' War.

It is said that the blueprints for the August Belmont Memorial Cup were first unveiled on the day of Hastings's Belmont Stakes victory. The trophy, which was commissioned by Belmont Jr. in memory of his father, was created by Paulding Farnham for Tiffany & Company using 350 ounces of sterling silver. Measuring eighteen inches in height and fourteen inches at the base, the trophy included an acorn-shaped bowl supported by three equine figurines; these represented Eclipse, Matchem and Herod, prominent grandsons of the foundation sires of the racing Thoroughbred. A statuette of the Belmont-owned Fenian, winner of the 1869 Belmont Stakes, stood atop the lid. The actual trophy was purportedly completed in time for the 1897 running of the race. According to author John Loring, Farnham created several additional trophies, which were presented to various Belmont Stakes winners during the period from 1897 to 1907. The original trophy would remain the property of the Belmont family until 1926, at which point it would be donated to the Westchester Racing Association as the permanent Belmont Stakes trophy.

By 1902, with the closure of Morris Park looming large, August Belmont Jr. sought to establish a new

The August Belmont trophy. *Library of Congress photo.*

37

racetrack. To that end, he partnered with William Collins Whitney to purchase a parcel of land to use for such a purpose. Whitney, an attorney, financier and secretary of the U.S. Navy, was a great benefactor to the sport of horse racing and was well known for his extreme generosity. According to a report by *Life* magazine:

> *One day, just to be nice, he called in a betting commissioner and explained that he wanted to bet $100 on his horse, Goldsmith, for each of the many guests he had brought with him to Saratoga—and $100 as well for each of the maids, waiters, clerks and bartenders who had served his party during its stay. The bet came to $12,000, and when Goldsmith won at six-to-one, Whitney became the most toasted host in Saratoga.*[7]

On another occasion, when his horse Volodyovski (whom he had leased from London socialite Lady Valerie Meux) won England's prestigious Epsom Derby in 1901, Whitney purchased champagne for everyone in attendance at Saratoga Race Course.

Whitney, like Belmont, was devoted to the cause of establishing a new racetrack in New York. Led by these two men, a new syndicate—which also included notables such as W.K. Vanderbilt, J.P. Morgan and James R. Keene—purchased 650 acres of land in Elmont, originally known as Foster's Meadow, on the border of Queens County and Nassau County.

William Collins Whitney. *Library of Congress photo.*

The parcel included Oatlands, a turreted Tudor-Gothic mansion (initially owned by the Manice family), which would serve as the track's Turf and Field Club until 1956.

The new racetrack, which Whitney suggested be named "Belmont Park" in honor of August Belmont I, was modeled after the great courses in England. As such, races would be run in a clockwise direction, so horses would finish directly in front of the clubhouse. This "reverse" direction, as compared with most American races, confused and frustrated early attendees. At the end of the inaugural spring meet, the *New York Tribune* wrote: "The scheme of running races the reverse way of the track, which the crowd insisted upon calling 'the wrong way,' had a tendency to confuse the spectators who were not accustomed to it, and threw them momentarily out of stride."[8] The practice would last fifteen years, at which point the races would be run counter-clockwise in keeping with American standards.

In addition to the direction of the races, the new track boasted other unique attributes. The oval-shaped dirt track (the "Main Track") measured one and a half miles in circumference, making it the largest in all of North America. For this reason, the dirt track would later earn the nickname "Big Sandy." The track was adjacent to a smaller training track, which was connected to it at the end. At the left end was a chute measuring one and a quarter miles, with a seven-furlong chute at the right end near the training track. A strip called the "Belmont Course" offered another route and also connected to the training track. On the inside of "Big Sandy" was a turf track, with a steeplechase course located farther on the inside.

The land on which Belmont Park was constructed had numerous trees, one of which—a large, Japanese white pine—would become an iconic figure in the years to come. According to a report by the New York Racing Association (NYRA), the tree dates back to 1826, long before the construction of the racetrack. Some sources assert that during the construction of Belmont Park, August Belmont Jr. and William Whitney arrived on site one day to find that many of the old trees were being cut down. According to these sources, the two men requested that certain of the trees be left on the property. The Japanese pine tree, situated in the paddock area, was therefore left standing. (In 1968, following construction of the new grandstand, the tree would become a part of the official Belmont Park logo.)

Early Belmont Park was quite charming in design, boasting several stone pillars and brass ornaments that had originally adorned the Washington Course at the South Carolina Jockey Club from 1792 to 1882. These were later presented as gifts to Belmont Park from the mayor and park

Early view of Big Sandy. *Library of Congress photo.*

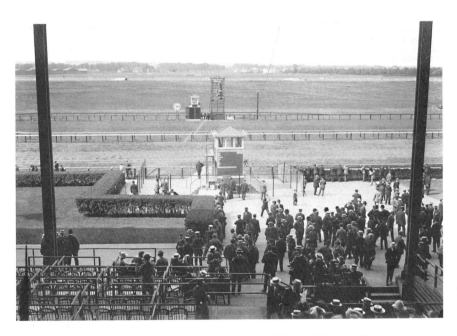

A view of the track and clocker's area in the early days. *Library of Congress photo.*

The Belmont Park clubhouse. *Library of Congress photo.*

commissioners of the city of Charleston. The pillars, along with a series of decorative iron railings from the grandstand, would be salvaged during renovations made in the 1960s and remain at Belmont Park today.

In addition to its aesthetic features, Belmont Park offered easy access for racegoers via the Long Island Rail Road extension from the Queens Village station, which ran along the borders of the property. This access to the railroad terminal simplified travel for folks from all social classes. The *New York Times* reported that, in the track's early days, "the attendance…was not restricted to any one locality nor to any one class. They came, men and women, old and young, from the classic confines of Boston and Cambridge, from Philadelphia and from the sporting environs of Chicago and the coast cities. The Bowery and the Avenue mingled in the surging democracy of the betting ring."[9]

The originally planned opening of Belmont Park was delayed by a year, owing to the death of William Whitney in February 1904. The track formally opened on Thursday, May 4, 1905, with a crowd of forty thousand in attendance. Newspaper reports from opening day reported that traffic was jammed heading into the entrance to the racecourse. The day's card included several key races, such as the Belmont Inaugural, which was won by

August Belmont Jr.'s Blandy, and the Met Mile, which ended in a dead heat between James R. Keene's Sysonby and his twenty-to-one challenger, Race King. Also in the Met Mile that day was Belmont's champion homebred filly, Beldame, the 1904 Horse of the Year.

The first Belmont Stakes run at the new park was held on the final day of the inaugural race meet. It proved a due cause for celebration, as William Whitney's homebred Tanya (now owned by his son, Harry Payne Whitney) became the second filly in history to win the race. A fancy chestnut with white socks and a blaze, Tanya captured the Belmont by a mere neck, completing the race in 2:08:00. The *New York Times* wrote:

> *The Belmont stood out as the feature of the program, chiefly on account of its great value. The race was one worthy of the stakes, the oldest turf fixture of the East, for it brought about a hotly fought finish between Tanya, post favorite, and Blandy, winner of the Withers. Tanya, which made about all the running, living only just long enough to get home first by a short neck, with all the others of the field of seven beaten off. The only other filly that has won a Belmont Stakes being Ruthless, which captured the event on its first running at Jerome Park in 1867.*[10]

Tanya, the winner of the 1905 Belmont Stakes. *Library of Congress photo.*

Following Tanya's victory, the Whitney family's prominence at Belmont Park would remain in full force. Harry Payne Whitney would return to the winner's circle the following year, when his colt, Burgomaster, captured the 1906 Belmont Stakes.

The early meetings at Belmont Park were deemed a sensation, with racegoers enjoying a series of thrilling finishes. The new facility attracted the sport's richest owners, who reveled in the challenge posted by the long and grueling Belmont dirt track. Despite its popularity, however, Big Sandy's dimensions had become a source of speculation, as the track's early races posted exceedingly fast times. According to racing historian Edward Bowen in the book *Belmont Park: A Century of Champions*, August Belmont took such matters into his proverbial own hands. Bowen wrote: "Annoyed, Belmont had S.H. McLaughlin, the chief surveyor for the Long Island Railroad, bring out a crew to remeasure various distances to the finish line. They were proven to be precise all along."[11]

With this evidence, the critics were silenced, and the sport of kings flourished at the new racecourse.

Chapter 6

EARLY YEARS

Belmont Park's early years were speckled with jubilation, and its races attracted the crème de la crème of New York's upper crust. In addition to flat racing, Belmont Park hosted various steeplechase events, in which horses galloped over a series of hurdles and water hazards in record time. From 1905 through 1958, Belmont Park would serve as the site of the American Grand National, which had originated at Morris Park over a steeplechase course spanning two and a half miles. According to the National Steeplechase Association, "They had all the jumping courses at Belmont, across Hempstead Avenue at what they called the Terminal, where the train used to come in. They had a timber course and every kind of fence imaginable. And there was jump racing every day."[12]

Whether the park was hosting flat races or steeplechase romps, Belmont's clubhouse in the early years hosted a virtual "who's who" of the area's high society. The Astors and Vanderbilts were frequent visitors, as were politicians, actors and sports personalities. Among the most colorful of Belmont's regular guests was James Buchanan Brady, nicknamed "Diamond Jim" due to his penchant for wearing opulent gems. Brady, together with his companion, actress Lillian Russell, threw frequent lavish parties at Belmont's Turf and Field Club. Diamond Jim spared no expense at these events, serving trays full of imported caviar, roast pheasant and Spanish oranges soaked in claret. According to legend, Brady's appetite was excessive, and he often consumed enough food for ten people in one sitting.

Mrs. Astor at the races. *Library of Congress photo.*

Mrs. Roosevelt at Belmont Park. *Library of Congress photo.*

"Diamond" Jim Brady (right). *Library of Congress photo.*

While Brady was entertaining guests in the Turf and Field Club, the racecourse continued to showcase the finest Thoroughbreds of the era. In 1907, James R. Keene's Peter Pan won the Belmont Stakes with a victory over the colt Frank Gill, which had previously defeated him in the Withers. Peter Pan's record that year included six wins and two seconds in nine attempts; his victories, in addition to the Belmont, included the Brooklyn Derby and the Brighton Handicap. A son of the 1901 Belmont Stakes winner, Commando, Peter Pan was later sold to a breeding farm in France for the sum of $100,000. The horse would eventually be purchased by Harry Payne Whitney and become the foundation stallion for Whitney Farm in Lexington, Kentucky.

One year after the triumph of Peter Pan, the team of Keene and Rowe added another Belmont Stakes to its growing list of victories. Colin, another son of the great Commando, dominated on the racetrack from his earliest start, winning his maiden race against twenty-three rivals in a virtual romp. The brown colt would retire undefeated after fifteen starts and would be widely recognized as one of the greatest horses ever to set foot on the track.

Interestingly, Rowe was reportedly unimpressed with Colin at first sight, as the colt had an oversized hock that the trainer mistook as a deformity. The

Peter Pan, winner of the 1907 Belmont Stakes. *Library of Congress photo.*

swelling did not appear to hinder the colt at all; three days after breaking his maiden, Colin smashed the existing track record for the National Stallion Stakes, a race that had originated in 1898 at Morris Park. In winning the Belmont Stakes the following season, Colin defeated, among others, August Belmont's stakes winner Fair Play. Author Kent Hollingsworth would later write of Colin, "Great horses have been beaten by mischance, racing luck, injury and lesser horses running the race of their lives. None of these, however, took Colin. He was unbeatable."[13] Colin's success was such that James Rowe requested that his own epitaph read, "He trained Colin."

While Colin was smashing records at the track, antigambling sentiments pervaded New York racing, and their effects were felt at Belmont Park. The Hart-Agnew Bill, also known as the "anti-racing law," was signed by Governor Charles Evans Hughes in June 1908. This bill, which deemed gambling at racetracks an illegal activity, was protested by August Belmont and Harry Payne Whitney. Despite their efforts, a subsequent bill, the Directors Criminal Liability

The Wright brothers at Belmont Park. *Library of Congress photo.*

Act, ensured that track board members would be fined and imprisoned for any gambling cited on their respective race grounds. This effectively resulted in the closure of New York racing facilities, and as such, there would be no Belmont Stakes run in 1911 or 1912. As a result, many prominent owners, including Belmont and Whitney, sent their horses to compete in England, and American jockeys left the United States to find work overseas.

During this hiatus from racing, Belmont Park lent its presence to another segment of U.S. history. In October 1910, the track hosted the International Aviation Tournament, a weeklong event staged by Wilbur and Orville Wright. The air show, which featured star aviator Glenn Curtiss in a race to the Statue of Liberty and back to Belmont Park, drew a crowd of more than 150,000 spectators who were mesmerized by this new form of air travel. In preparation for this event, the *New York Times* wrote: "Belmont Park is now ready for the aviators. After six weeks' work the race course has

Belmont Park aviation meet, October 1910. *Library of Congress photo.*

Belmont Park air show, October 1910. *Library of Congress photo.*

been transformed into one of the finest aviation fields in the world. The posts, rails, trees, and other obstructions have been removed, and the field resembles a well-kept grass plot. The extra boxes have been completed and the parking spaces for automobiles arranged."[14]

In 1913, a New York court ruled that the Hart-Agnew Law was not relevant to oral betting, and racing was therefore allowed to resume.

A race in 1913. *Library of Congress photo.*

Several area tracks, including Coney Island's Brighton Beach Race Course, Gravesend Race Track and Sheepshead Bay Race Track, would never be reopened. Fortunately, Belmont Park was not one of that number, and the track opened its gates amid great fanfare on May 30, 1913. On that day, Harry Payne Whitney's six-year-old stallion, Whisk Broom II, won the Met Mile in what was his first race in the United States and also his earliest running on dirt. Carrying 120 pounds, the stallion came from behind to defeat Meridian by one length as a crowd of twenty thousand cheered in the stands. Later that season, Whisk Broom II became the first horse to capture the New York Handicap Triple Crown, which included the Met Mile, the Suburban Handicap and the Brooklyn Handicap. Only three other horses to date have equaled this feat.

In 1916, August Belmont won the first of two consecutive Belmont Stakes races with the victory of the chestnut colt Friar Rock. A son of the 1903 English Triple Crown champion Rock Sand, which Belmont had purchased and imported to the United States, Friar Rock was foaled at Nursery Stud's Lexington, Kentucky stable. Friar Rock's dam, Fairy Gold, would also produce the notorious Fair Play.

Friar Rock began his career as a two-year-old, earning wins in the Whirl Stakes and the Adirondack Stakes at Saratoga. The following season, the colt dominated on the track. In addition to the Belmont Stakes, he captured the Brooklyn Handicap, the Suburban Handicap and the Saratoga Cup, en route to earning Horse of the Year honors.

August Belmont returned to the winner's circle in 1917, as another homebred colt, Hourless, won the Belmont Stakes. The colt had been bred at Belmont's Normandy-based operation and foaled in England. In 1915, as World War I spread in Europe, Belmont shipped both Hourless and his dam, Hour Glass, to the United States.

Hourless won several races as a two-year-old, including Saratoga's premier juvenile races, the Hopeful and Grand Union Hotel Stakes. The following season, Belmont opted to forego the Kentucky Derby and the Preakness (which, incidentally, were held on the same day that year) and point Hourless toward the longer-distance Belmont Stakes. Hourless won the Withers Stakes at Aqueduct and then headed to Big Sandy, where he set a new record at one and three-eighths miles in capturing the Belmont trophy for his owner.

That same year, Belmont Park introduced the Coaching Club American Oaks, a race for fillies modeled after the Epsom Oaks in England. The race was named for the Coaching Club of America, in which August Belmont and other prominent owners, such as Belair Stud's William Woodward Sr., were members. Prospective members of the Coaching Club were asked to prove their ability by handling a coach and four horses with a single set of reins. The Coaching Club American Oaks, which would become a premier race for three-year-old fillies, would be held at Belmont Park for many years. The winner of the inaugural running, at nine furlongs, was the filly Wistful I.

Prior to the start of the 1917 spring meeting, Belmont Park was the unfortunate target of suspected arson. On April 14, the lavish grandstand was burned to the ground, resulting in more than $1 million worth of damage. Several days later, more than twenty-four horses tragically perished when another fire raged through an area of the stables. Police determined that foul play was involved in both incidents but never made an arrest. However, at that point, the Pinkerton National Detective Agency was hired to safeguard Belmont Park from would-be arsonists and other criminals. While activity at the racetrack resumed after the fires, major construction was required to restore Belmont Park to its original splendor. In the meantime, temporary structures were utilized to continue Belmont Park's operations during this period.

Aside from racing, Belmont Park once again made history when it served as the area terminal for the first airmail service between New York and Washington, D.C. The first scheduled U.S. Air Mail service began on May

15, 1918, with U.S. Army pilots flying Curtiss JN-4HM "Jenny" biplanes. The planes originated at the Washington Polo Grounds and flew to Belmont Park, with a stop made at Bustleton Field in Philadelphia.

Meanwhile, racing continued on its regular schedule, with new events periodically added to the card. In 1919, the Jockey Club Stakes, which would later become known as the Jockey Club Gold Cup, was established at Belmont Park. Open to horses of either sex, aged three years and up, the race was originally run at a distance of one and a half miles on the dirt. The inaugural running was won in a walkover by Glen Riddle Farm's Purchase, a horse that was nicknamed the "Adonis of the Turf" due to his exceptional good looks. In later years, the Jockey Club Gold Cup would serve as the main draw for the fall meeting, attracting the best three-year-olds, as well as older horses, on a weight-for-age basis.

DISTANCE OF THE JOCKEY CLUB GOLD CUP	
Years	**Distance**
1919, 1920	One and a half miles
1921–1975	Two miles
1976–1989	One and a half miles
1990–present	One and a quarter miles

The year 1919 also witnessed the brilliance of the colt Sir Barton, a three-year-old chestnut with a mercurial temperament. Sir Barton had begun an unimpressive juvenile season for owner John E. Madden during the prior year. When the horse failed to win a single race out of six juvenile starts, Madden sold Sir Barton to Canadian businessman J.K.L. Ross for $10,000. Ross, in turn, sent the horse to trainer H. Guy Bedwell in preparation for the colt's three-year-old season.

Sir Barton, without a single win to his credit, was entered in the 1919 Kentucky Derby solely as a "rabbit" (or pacemaker) for his favored stablemate, the colt Billy Kelly. To the surprise of both owner and trainer, Sir Barton led the field of twelve horses from wire to wire, ultimately winning the Derby by five lengths. He returned to the track a mere four days later to win the Preakness Stakes at Pimlico in a four-length, wire-to-wire romp. After capturing the Withers Stakes at Aqueduct, Sir Barton proceeded to set an American record at the one-and-three-eighths distance in winning the 1919 Belmont Stakes. While the Derby, Preakness and Belmont would later become known collectively as the Triple Crown, there was no such

Sir Barton, the first winner of the Triple Crown series. *Library of Congress photo.*

distinction at that time. As there was no incentive for winning all three, owners did not always enter the same horses in the series of races.

Eleven years would pass before the phrase "Triple Crown" would be identified, and Sir Barton would be recognized as the first to have accomplished the outstanding feat. But in 1919, while Sir Barton was racing, the eyes of the public were squarely focused on another valiant colt. This horse, bred by August Belmont Jr., was a two-year-old chestnut with an ivory star and a massive girth. Over the next few months, his name would become legendary on the hallowed track at Belmont Park.

Chapter 7

NURSERY STUD'S "MOSTEST HOSS"

On March 29, 1917, the homebred mare Mahubah foaled a sturdy chestnut colt at the stables of August Belmont's Nursery Stud. Sired by Fair Play, and carrying the bloodlines of British Triple Crown winner Rock Sand, the colt was bred for distance running. While Belmont originally had high aspirations for this colt, he had more weighty matters on his mind at this time. Now in his sixties, he had volunteered for military service at the onset of World War I and had been stationed, worlds away, in France.

At the time of his military service, Belmont was celebrating his seventh year of marriage to the former Broadway actress Eleanor Robson. Mrs. Belmont had married August Jr. in 1910, more than twelve years after the death of his first wife, Elizabeth. Under her maiden name, Mrs. Belmont had performed various coveted stage roles, including Salomy Jane and Shakespeare's Juliet.

It was a family tradition for Mrs. Belmont, rather than her husband, to name the Nursery Stud foals. When it came time to christen the Mahubah colt, Mrs. Belmont dubbed him "My Man o' War" as a tribute to her military husband. At some point, the word "My" was dropped from the colt's Jockey Club papers, and the horse was officially registered as "Man o' War."

Major Belmont had always been largely involved in the training of his horses, yet he was limited while stationed in France in 1918. Under these circumstances, he was prompted for the first time to sell his crop of yearlings at the annual Saratoga auction. According to sources, this plan did not originally include Man o' War; Belmont had intended to keep the

Eleanor Belmont, wife of August Belmont Jr. *Library of Congress photo.*

finest colt for himself. In the end, however, Belmont felt that it was not in his best interest to retain possession of the young horse. When Belmont was unable to sell the Nursery Stud yearlings as a package, the decision was made to sell them at Saratoga individually. Man o' War was thus shipped to Saratoga to be sold with the other Nursery Stud yearlings on August 17, 1918.

Trainer Louis Feustel was familiar with Nursery Stud, as he had worked for the Belmont stables for many years. He had, in fact, trained Mahubah and had galloped the fiery and volatile Hastings. When Belmont joined the army, however, there was little work for Feustel at Nursery Stud, so the trainer sought work elsewhere. By 1918, Feustel was the head trainer at Glen Riddle Farms in Pennsylvania, owned by textile manufacturer Samuel Riddle. According to an interview with the trainer shortly before his death, Feustel had urged his boss to purchase the entire crop of Belmont yearlings the month prior to the Saratoga auction. Feustel was particularly smitten with the young Man o' War. It is said, however, that Riddle himself was not duly impressed with the colt.

When the auction date arrived, Riddle and his wife attended and purchased several of the Belmont colts. At the urging of his wife and Feustel, Riddle purchased Man o' War for $5,000. Riddle's alleged reasoning was that the colt could be trained as a field hunter if he proved unsuccessful at the track. While $5,000 was well above the average price of $1,107 for colts sold at the auction that year, Man o' War did not command the highest price. That distinction went to a chestnut colt with a white blaze named Golden Broom, which was purchased by Riddle's cousin Sarah Jeffords. Incidentally, the man who did the actual bidding on Man o' War was not Riddle himself but his friend Ed Buehler. The latter's nephew, Richard Stone Reeves, would go on to become one of the most famous painters of Thoroughbred horses in modern history.

Man o' War inherited much of his grandsire's hot temperament and proved difficult to break and train. He progressed, however, under Feustel's patience and steady hand. The colt, nicknamed "Big Red," began his race career at Belmont Park, easily breaking his maiden in a six-length romp over the competition. Three days later, Man o' War returned to Big Sandy, where he won the Keene Memorial Stakes by three lengths over On Watch (sired by the great Colin) in 1:05:60 over five and a half furlongs. Belmont Park would in fact become the site of many of Man o' War's victories.

The colt continued the season with wins at Aqueduct and Saratoga before sustaining his only career loss in Saratoga's Sanford Stakes, which most believe was due solely to an error by his jockey. By the time of his win in the Hopeful Stakes at the Spa, the colt was being compared to great horses such as Colin and Sysonby. Fans were impressed by Man o' War's effortless stamina and his apparent ease in carrying weights of up to 130 pounds.

Man o' War returned to Belmont Park for the fall meet, where he bested Harry Payne Whitney's horse, John P. Grier, by two and a half lengths in the Futurity Stakes. The race, commonly known as the "Belmont Futurity," had originated in 1888 at the Sheepshead Bay Racetrack. Following the closure of Sheepshead Bay, the race was moved to Saratoga before being relocated to Belmont Park in 1915. Reportedly, until 1956, the Futurity Stakes offered a larger purse than the Belmont Stakes.

Following his victory in the Futurity, Man o' War would remain undefeated, setting various records in the process. Contrary to popular belief, Man o' War did not compete in the Kentucky Derby, as Riddle believed that the mile and a quarter was too much for a young three-year-old so early in the season. At Pimlico, Man o' War easily won the Preakness Stakes over Upset (which, coincidentally, had handed the colt his only career defeat) before heading back to Belmont Park. Big Red won the Belmont Stakes by an astounding twenty lengths, setting a speed record that would remain for fifty years.

Man o' War's brilliance intimidated the most confident of horse owners, and few wished for their animals to face him on the track. On September 4, 1920, he dominated the Lawrence Realization Stakes at Belmont, besting his only other competitor—the Jeffords' horse, Hoodwink—by more than one hundred lengths. In the process, Big Red set yet another world record, blazing the mile and five-eighths in 2:40:80. The Lawrence Realization Stakes, originally run on the turf, was held at Sheepshead Bay from 1899 through 1913 before moving to the dirt track at Belmont Park.

Man o' War returned to Big Sandy for the Jockey Club Stakes (later known as the Jockey Club Gold Cup), where he defeated Harry Payne Whitney's

The immortal Man o' War. *Photo courtesy Keeneland Library.*

Damask—his sole competitor in the race—by fifteen lengths in a time of 2:28:80, smashing the track record for a mile and a half while under tight restraint by jockey Clarence Kummer. According to sources, Whitney likely entered his horse in a gesture of sportsmanship to ensure that Big Red would at least have one competitor.

Following his stellar performances at Belmont Park, Man o' War galloped to victory in the Potomac Handicap at Havre de Grace Racetrack in Maryland, where he set a track record while carrying 138 pounds. He finished the season with a celebrated victory over Sir Barton in a match race at Canada's Kenilworth Park.

By the time he retired following his victory over Sir Barton, Big Red had amassed twenty wins in twenty-one starts, set numerous track records and earned himself a place in history as perhaps the greatest racehorse of all time. Joe Palmer, legendary turf writer and historian, would later write of Man o' War:

> *He did not beat, he merely annihilated. He did not run to world records, he galloped to them. He was so far superior to his contemporaries that,*

except for one race against John P. Grier, they could not extend him. In 1920 he dominated racing as perhaps no athlete—not Tilden or Jones or Dempsey or Louis or Nurmi or Thorpe or any human athlete—had dominated his sport. [15]

Yet perhaps the greatest description of Man o' War was attributed to his longtime groom, Will Harbut, who dubbed him the "mostest hoss that ever was."

Chapter 8

THE ROARING TWENTIES

By the time Man o' War made his final victory lap, Belmont Park had undergone a major renovation. The grandstand, which had been ravaged by fire in 1917, was rebuilt at a much larger size in order to comfortably seat 17,500 patrons. The *New York Times* heralded the upcoming reconstruction, noting that "when the changes in the track proper, the clubhouse, grandstand and paddocks shall have been completed, Belmont Park will be the most magnificently appointed racing plant on the American continent."[16]

By 1921, the track itself had changed, as the one-and-a-quarter-mile chute had been moved to the upper right of the backstretch area. Beginning in 1921, the park had abandoned its practice of British-style clockwise racing, which had been unpopular with many owners and spectators. When Grey Lag won the 1921 Belmont Stakes, the race was run counter-clockwise for the very first time.

At this time, America was in the midst of the Roaring Twenties, a decade of great celebration and prosperity. It was the golden age of horse racing, and Americans flocked to the track to celebrate their equine heroes. The colt Mad Hatter became the first multiple winner of the Jockey Club Gold Cup when he won consecutive runnings of the two-mile race in 1921 and 1922. Mad Hatter, a son of Fair Play, had been bred by August Belmont Jr. and was a full brother to 1924 Belmont Stakes winner Mad Play. In addition to the Gold Cup, Mad Hatter won consecutive runnings of the Metropolitan Handicap in 1921 and 1922.

In 1923, Belmont Park became the site of one of the most anticipated events of the era when it hosted a match race between Kentucky Derby winner Zev and Epsom Derby champion Papyrus. On October 20, a crowd of nearly fifty thousand spectators flocked to Belmont Park to watch Zev handily outrun the British champion by a full five lengths. The American champ, named in honor of lawyer Colonel J.W. Zevely, was owned by oil magnate Harry F. Sinclair. Zev's other key victories at Big Sandy—the Belmont Stakes and the Lawrence Realization—helped earn him Horse of the Year honors that season. Zev would retire the following year as the sport's all-time leading money earner, a record that was previously held by the immortal Man o' War.

As new records were being set at Belmont Park, the aging August Belmont Jr. continued to oversee its operations. Additionally, while no longer actively campaigning his horses, he had remained active in the management of Nursery Stud. At the age of seventy-one, however, Belmont fell ill in his office. Despite being rushed into surgery, Belmont developed blood poisoning and slipped into a coma. He died on December 10, 1924, a mere thirty-six hours after becoming ill. Belmont's funeral was held in New York, after which his body was interred in the Belmont family plot at Island Cemetery in Newport, Rhode Island. After his death, Belmont's widow sold the majority of her husband's estate to a property developer. A substantial portion of Nursery Stud's breeding stock was sold to a partnership that included Joseph Widener, W. Averell Harriman and George Herbert Walker (grandfather of later U.S. president George H.W. Bush). Among the horses acquired at this time were Man o' War's sire and dam, Fair Play and Mahubah; Chance Shot, a son of Fair Play, which would go on to win the Belmont Stakes in 1927; and Chance Play, which would win the Jockey Club Gold Cup that same year.

During his lifetime, Belmont Jr. was highly praised in the racing industry for his many great contributions to the sport. *TIME* magazine, in a report of his death, referred to Belmont Jr. as "the leading turf man in the U.S." and, in fact, credited him with saving New York racing. In addition to the founding and operation of Belmont Park, he was a noted breeder of both racehorses and polo ponies, the latter infused with Thoroughbred blood from the stallion Kentucky. During his lifetime, the distinctive Belmont silks—black with bright red sleeves—were carried to numerous stakes wins, both in the United States and overseas.

Belmont was succeeded as president of the Westchester Racing Association, which operated Belmont Park, by horseman Joseph E. Widener, who had purchased the above-referenced Nursery Stud stock. A wealthy Philadelphian, Widener would serve as the racetrack's president until 1939.

August Belmont Jr. (*right*) with friend Paul Cravath. *Library of Congress photo.*

He was a founding benefactor of Washington's National Gallery of Art and a prominent Thoroughbred horse owner who would win back-to-back runnings of the Belmont Stakes in 1933 and 1934 with Hurryoff and Peace Chance, respectively. Widener maintained substantial breeding operations for both flat racers and steeplechase horses at his Elmendorf Farm in Kentucky; two of his steeplechasers were eventually elected to the U.S. Racing Hall of Fame. In addition to his association with Belmont Park, Widener would later establish the famed Hialeah Park racetrack in Miami, Florida.

Under the guidance of Widener, several renovations were made at Belmont Park. These included the introduction of the Widener Chute in 1926, a seven-furlong diagonal extension from the training track to the upper part of the homestretch. The chute would be discarded in 1958 as it fell out of favor, and the name "Widener" would later be affixed to one of the racetrack's outer turf courses.

Despite the death of its founder, racing at Belmont Park continued with great success throughout the latter part of the 1920s. Belmont-bred horses garnered great success for their new owners during this time. Chance Play, then owned solely by Averell Harriman, captured the 1927 Jockey Club Gold Cup as part of a stellar four-year-old season. While the colt had won the six-furlong Campfire Handicap at Belmont Park as a three-year-old, his potential as a distance horse was questionable, and he was not entered in any of the major spring races. The following autumn, the colt rallied to win the mile-and-a-sixteenth Potomac Handicap in Maryland and came into his own during the following season. In addition to the Jockey Club Gold Cup, Chance Play's wins in 1927 included the Merchants and Citizens Handicap at Saratoga and the Toboggan Handicap at Aqueduct.

That season, spectators at Belmont Park witnessed a controversial finish when the filly Anita Peabody defeated her favored stablemate, Reigh Count, at the wire in the Futurity Stakes. The colt maintained the lead approaching the finish line when the filly suddenly passed him by the slimmest of margins to take the win. A photographer for the *New York Times* captured a fascinating photo of the final moment of the race, in which the two jockeys stared at each other while crossing the wire. It is unknown whether the upset was due to jockey error or to instructions from John and Fannie Hertz, who owned both horses.

Reigh Count went on to avenge his Futurity loss, dominating the sport during his three-year-old season. After winning the Kentucky Derby in May, the colt was sidelined from the Preakness and Belmont Stakes due to injury. A healthy Reigh Count returned to racing that summer, defeating Preakness champion Victorian in the Lawrence Realization and winning the Jockey Club Gold Cup over several older horses. Reigh Count subsequently raced as a four-year-old in England, where he won the illustrious Coronation Cup at Epsom Racecourse.

According to *TIME* magazine, owner John Hertz once refused an offer of $1 million for the dark-colored colt. The decision worked out well for Hertz, as Reigh Count went on to sire Triple Crown winner Count Fleet. Amusingly, Hertz allegedly had purchased Reigh Count after seeing him bite another horse during a race; Hertz was supposedly impressed by the act, deeming the horse "a fighter."

The Roaring Twenties was a time of prosperity, and its effects were evident in the horse racing scene. The decade, ushered in by the immortal Man o' War, introduced a bevy of outstanding horses at Belmont Park. The years of good fortune benefited the sport, as folks spent freely at the betting tables. Unfortunately, the fate of America was about to change, and in late October 1929, the U.S. Stock Market sustained a shocking crash. "Black Tuesday," as it came to be known, heralded the start of the Great Depression, which would have a devastating impact on the country for the next ten years. During this period, millions of people lost their jobs, and the celebration of the prior decade faded to a distant memory.

America was very much in need of a hero.

Chapter 9

THE REIGN OF BELAIR STUD

When Sir Barton, winner of the Derby and Preakness, crossed the finish line in the 1919 Belmont Stakes, there was no mention of a "Triple Crown." That phrase would not be coined until many years later, when a superstar colt by the name of Gallant Fox arrived on the scene. Gallant Fox became a hero when America was at its lowest peak, and his prominence brought a sense of hope to racing fans throughout the nation.

"The Fox of Belair," as he came to be known, was the result of careful breeding by owner William Woodward Sr. A contemporary and friend of August Belmont Jr., Woodward had studied the bloodlines of English champions in an effort to introduce greater stamina into the American Thoroughbred. At his Belair Stud farm in Bowie, Maryland, Woodward bred for distance, aiming toward his lifetime goal of winning the esteemed Epsom Derby. While it served as the model for the Kentucky Derby, the Epsom was a longer race, with horses racing one and a half miles over grueling British terrain. Because of that goal, among American races, Woodward favored the Belmont Stakes due to its increased distance.

Gallant Fox was a son of the imported French stallion Sir Gallahad II, out of Woodward's beloved mare Marguerite. The colt was an attractive bay with a wide blaze and splashes of ivory above all four hooves. He also had a "wall eye," a condition in which the iris lacks pigment and is surrounded by a light ring. According to some sources, Woodward believed that Gallant Fox's optical defect would provide a distinct advantage on the racetrack, as other horses would be frightened and unwilling to pass the colt with the "evil eye."

Belair Stud's Gallant Fox, 1930 Triple Crown champion. *Photo courtesy Belair Stable Museum.*

Gallant Fox followed the typical schedule of Woodward's Belair Stud program. He was foaled at Claiborne Farm in Kentucky and shipped to Belair Stud as a weanling. After earning the approval of Woodward and trainer James "Sunny Jim" Fitzsimmons, the colt completed his early schooling and was shipped to Aqueduct for training.

Gallant Fox was an amiable horse that enjoyed the company of humans; among his other traits, however, were laziness and a lack of attention. This became apparent when he began his racing career with less than stellar results. The colt failed to impress in his first two races, much to the dismay of both owner and trainer. In his next start in Belmont Park's Tremont Stakes, Gallant Fox frustrated the Belair Stud team when he placed a disappointing eighth. The frustration was magnified because the loss had nothing to do with the colt's talent. As the race began, Gallant Fox was so preoccupied by the sounds of an airplane flying overhead that he failed to break with the other starters and fell miserably behind.

The Tremont was to be Gallant Fox's only career finish out of the money. He broke his maiden in his next start in late July at Saratoga and placed second at the Spa in the U.S. Hotel Stakes. The Fox was then shipped back

Belair Stud's William Woodward (at right) and "Sunny" Jim Fizsimmons. *Photo courtesy Belair Stable Museum.*

to Belmont for the Futurity Trial, where he overcame traffic to come within a neck of the win. He returned to Big Sandy for the Belmont Futurity, where he placed a game third behind the eventual juvenile champion, Whichone, owned by Harry Payne Whitney. Gallant Fox made his final juvenile start in the Junior Champion Stakes at Aqueduct, and the dazzling colt made the race his own. He defeated the eventual Kentucky Jockey Club Stakes winner Desert Light by two lengths, despite carrying five additional pounds.

Gallant Fox matured in the off-season, pleasing both owner and trainer. Having never had the benefit of a regular rider, the horse was matched with jockey Earl Sande for the 1930 season. The pair triumphed in the Wood Memorial at Jamaica prior to winning the Preakness Stakes, which was at that time held in advance of the Kentucky Derby. From Pimlico it was on to Churchill Downs, where days of pelting rain had rendered the dirt track sloppy. The Fox of Belair handled this challenge like a champion. Breaking well from the gate, the colt was boxed in close quarters for the first three-eighths of a mile before taking the lead for the duration of the race.

Following his Derby win, Gallant Fox headed to Belmont Park, where he would face a new set of challenges. Whichone, which had been sidelined with an injury that had kept him out of both the Preakness and the Derby, was back in great form. Whitney's colt, appearing sleek and ready for battle, had just come off a four-length victory in the Withers Stakes at Aqueduct and was, in fact, sent off as the top betting choice. Another challenge would be posed by Earl Sande's physical state. Two nights prior to the Belmont

Owner William Woodward leads Gallant Fox at Belmont. *Photo courtesy Belair Stable Museum.*

Stakes, Sande had been a passenger in an automobile accident and had sustained several injuries to his face and hands.

Sande had overcome numerous obstacles in his life and was not about to give up easily. He gave the race his best effort, guiding Gallant Fox in a wire-to-wire victory over rival Whichone and multiple stakes winner Questionnaire. With this victory, Gallant Fox became the all-time leading money winner to date.

Interestingly, while Sir Barton had won the Derby, Preakness and Belmont Stakes in 1919, it was Gallant Fox's capture of the trio of races that led to the coinage of the phrase Triple Crown. Charles Hatton of the *Daily Racing Form* is typically credited with the first reference to a "Triple Crown" in describing Gallant Fox's sweep of the three races. Around that same time, Bryan Field, a columnist for the *New York Times*, wrote: "Earl Sande gave all the credit to his mount which by winning the Preakness, Kentucky Derby, and Belmont had equaled the feat of Sir Barton. These two horses are the only ones to win the 'Triple Crown.'"[17]

After handing Belair Stud its first Triple Crown, Gallant Fox continued his winning ways, capturing the Dwyer Stakes at Belmont Park and besting Derby runner-up Gallant Knight by a neck in Chicago's Arlington Classic. By that time, Gallant Fox had been lauded as one of the sport's all-time greats, with the *Boston Globe* referring to him as "America's greatest race horse since Man o' War."

During the summer, the Fox of Belair was shockingly upset by a colt called Jim Dandy in the Travers at Saratoga but rebounded to defeat older horses in the Saratoga Cup. He then headed back to Big Sandy for a win in the Lawrence Realization at one and five-eighths miles. The Fox completed his classic season at Belmont in the grueling two-mile Jockey Club Gold Cup, solidifying his position as both champion three-year-old colt and Horse of the Year. With continued comparisons to Man o' War and other immortals, Gallant Fox's accomplishments had placed him in elite company. In September 1930, Colonel Walter Moriarty of the *National Turf Digest* wrote: "Few horses in any country have really earned the right to be called 'great'… Gallant Fox is a great horse. If he never wins another race, he will go down in history as one of the best ever bred in any country."[18]

Following the retirement of Gallant Fox at season's end, William Woodward continued to garner success at Belmont Park. In 1932, Belair Stud boasted its second Belmont Stakes winner with the victory of the colt Faireno. Foaled at Claiborne Farm in 1929, the brawny bay was sired by Chatterton (a son of Fair Play) out of the mare Minerva. Faireno had some success as a two-year-old, winning races such as the Nursery Handicap for juveniles at Belmont Park. However, his three-year-old season had started out badly, prompting Woodward to keep him out of the Kentucky Derby. The horse was shipped to Pimlico instead, but Woodward and Fitzsimmons were unimpressed with his training efforts. Rather than entering him in the Preakness, Woodward opted for the Campfire Purse at Belmont, where the colt made a strong showing in preparation for the upcoming Belmont Stakes. This strategy proved to be successful for Woodward, and Faireno led virtually wire-to-wire in bringing a second Belmont trophy back to Belair Stud.

After his Belmont Stakes victory, Faireno won key races at various tracks before returning to Big Sandy for a victory in the Lawrence Realization. Sadly, the colt sustained a tendon injury during this race that would sideline him for more than a year. Nevertheless, at season's end, Faireno shared champion three-year-old male honors with Kentucky Derby champion Burgoo King.

While Woodward was celebrating the success of Faireno, a new youngster was galloping in the Belair Stud pastures. Triple Crown winner Gallant Fox, in his first foal crop, had sired a leggy chestnut colt out of the mare Flambino. A daughter of the British champion Wrack, Flambino had been a successful racer in her own right. In 1927, she won the Gazelle Stakes at Aqueduct and placed a well-respected third in the Belmont Stakes.

The new colt was flashy like his sire, with splashes of white on both hind legs and a handsome wide blaze. William Woodward had traced the colt's lineage back to the stallion Ormonde* (winner of the Epsom Derby) and desired a name that also began with the letter *o*. According to sources, "Omaha" was the first name that came to Mr. Woodward's mind, and the colt was named accordingly. Contrary to popular belief, the colt was not named for the city of Omaha, Nebraska.

Omaha began his racing career with a disappointing loss on June 18, 1934, beaten by a mere nose in his first outing. Five days later, the lanky colt was in winning form, breaking his maiden in a five-furlong allowance race at Aqueduct. While hopes were high for the son of Gallant Fox, Omaha was yet to triumph again as a two-year-old. After being winless at Saratoga that summer, Omaha was shipped to Belmont Park for the Champagne Stakes. Despite performing well over the grueling Big Sandy track, Omaha lost in a photo finish to the eventual juvenile champion Balladier, which galloped away with a new track record. Omaha then put in a disappointing performance in the Belmont Futurity before rebounding to place second in the Junior Champion Stakes at Aqueduct. By season end, however, the son of Gallant Fox had finished out of the money in four of his nine starts.

Omaha, the "Belair Bullet." *Photo courtesy Belair Stable Museum.*

Over the winter months, the once lanky Omaha began to fill out and suddenly took on the appearance of a champion. At close to seventeen hands, he was larger than his sire. According to sources, Omaha's size often required a double stall in order for the horse to be comfortable. To accomplish this, many racetracks were forced to remove the partition between two existing stalls to accommodate the large colt.

Omaha began his three-year-old season with a win in an overnight allowance race at Aqueduct and then finished a game third behind Today and Plat Eye in the Wood Memorial under Canadian jockey Willie "Smokey" Saunders. After his solid finish in the Wood Memorial, the colt headed to the Triple Crown races that had been won by his sire a mere five years earlier. By this time, the Kentucky Derby at Churchill Downs was the first of the three races in the series. Omaha was sent off as the second betting choice, with Calumet Farm's Nellie Flag deemed the odds-on favorite to don the garland of roses. Nellie Flag was piloted by nineteen-year-old Eddie Arcaro, who was riding in his first-ever Kentucky Derby.

Despite the public's high hopes for Nellie Flag, the filly was to finish out of the money. Soaring across the hallowed dirt at Churchill Downs, Omaha galloped from the outside post to gain the lead, winning by one and a half lengths over Roman Soldier and Whiskolo. Following Omaha's Derby win, the media swarmed around William Woodward, questioning the Master of Belair for his predictions on the coming races. The eloquent Woodward simply responded that he hoped Omaha "would be just like" his sire.

In the Preakness Stakes the following week, Omaha showed that comparisons to his sire were warranted, as he won by six lengths over Mr. and Mrs. Walter Jeffords' colt Firethorn and Hopeful Stakes champion Psychic Bid. However, a loss in the Withers Stakes at Aqueduct gave fodder to some of Omaha's critics, who felt that the colt was not equipped to handle the longer distance of the Belmont Stakes.

Four contenders took to a rain-soaked track at Belmont to try to prevent Omaha from winning the Triple Crown. Among them was the popular Rosemont, which had defeated Omaha in the Withers (and would later conquer Seabiscuit in the Santa Anita Handicap). As the gate opened, the early lead went to Alfred G. Vanderbilt's Cold Shoulder, which was passed in approaching the stretch run by a driving Firethorn. In a thrilling finish, Omaha passed the brown Sun Briar colt, winning the race by one and a half lengths and duplicating his sire's great feat in winning the Triple Crown for Belair. The *Blood Horse* wrote:

> *Amid hearty cheering, Saunders brought Omaha back to the winner's circle, the victory being the most popular of the day. There, despite a driving rain, waited Omaha's owner, William Woodward, and the New York banker led in, for the second time in his Turf career, a horse which had won the Kentucky Derby, Preakness and Belmont Stakes in his colors. The first, in 1930, was Gallant Fox, sire of the present 3-year-old champion, now indisputably at the top of his division.*[19]

Omaha's blistering bursts of speed impressed racegoers and media alike, who nicknamed the striking chestnut the "Belair Bullet." The season ended with disappointment, however, when Omaha was injured during a pre-Travers workout at Saratoga and was forced to retire for the remainder of the season. In a further disappointment for Woodward and Belair Stud, the colt Discovery—and not Omaha—was named Horse of the Year at season's end. Discovery, known as the "Iron Horse" for carrying weights of up to 139 pounds, had won eleven of nineteen starts that season. (To date, this would

Triple Crown winner Omaha with owner William Woodward. *Photo courtesy Belair Stable Museum.*

be the only instance in which a Triple Crown winner would fail to be named Horse of the Year.)

Omaha's sweep of the Triple Crown races earned Belair Stud a prominent place in history. At the very moment in which Omaha crossed

Granville, winner of the 1936 Belmont Stakes. *Photo courtesy Belair Stable Museum.*

the finish line at Belmont, Belair Stud became the only owner/breeder to produce father-son Triple Crown champions. As of this writing, that feat has yet to be duplicated.

Belair Stud's success over the Belmont track continued into the following year, when the colt Granville brought Woodward his second consecutive—and fourth overall—Belmont Stakes trophy. While hopes were high for this strapping son of Gallant Fox, Granville's juvenile season was disappointing, as the colt won only one of his seven starts. His best finish was a third-place showing in the 1935 Champagne Stakes at Belmont, a race that was won by Joseph Widener's colt, Brevity.

Showing promise in his three-year-old season, Granville seemed to be held back only by a string of bad luck. He finished second in a photo finish behind Teufel in the Wood Memorial, then stumbled and fell to his knees in the early moments of the Kentucky Derby, tossing jockey James Stout and forcing his own elimination from the Run for the Roses. Granville then lost the Preakness by a nose to the Derby champion, Bold Venture. At last, fate seemed to be on his side at Big Sandy when he defeated Dwyer Stakes champion Mr. Bones by the smallest winning margin—a nose—in the Belmont Stakes. After winning several other key races, Granville returned to Belmont Park for a victory in the Lawrence Realization over one mile and five-eighths, proving that he was indeed a distance horse.

In eleven starts as a three-year-old, Granville had amassed seven wins and three seconds, earning championship honors as the top three-year-old colt. When formal voting was implemented by the *Daily Racing Form* in 1936, Granville became the first to be voted Horse of the Year. At the end of his championship season, however, the colt sustained an ankle injury that led to his retirement. Unfortunately, he did not stamp his offspring with talent and was ultimately disappointing as a sire.

Granville's retirement was not the end of the line for Woodward, whose colt Johnstown captured the 1939 Belmont Stakes—the fifth such win for Belair Stud in a single decade. Bred by Arthur Hancock, Johnstown had been privately purchased as a yearling by Woodward. After winning the Kentucky Derby in thrilling style, the lop-eared "Big John" struggled over

Johnstown, 1939 Belmont Stakes winner. *Photo courtesy Belair Stable Museum.*

a muddy track at Pimlico, fading to fifth in the Preakness Stakes. Like most Belair horses, however, he relished the added distance of the Belmont Stakes, topping a field of six starters in an easy triumph over the colt Belay.

Woodward's success at Belmont Park would continue in the years to come. Following his death, many years later, in 1954, the Woodward Stakes would be inaugurated in his honor. "The Woodward" would originate at Aqueduct and later move to Belmont Park before eventually being relocated to Saratoga in 2006. Befitting the great man for whom it was named, the Woodward Stakes would showcase the nation's most illustrious Thoroughbred champions.

Chapter 10

A Decade of
Triple Crown Wins

Nestled between the victories of Granville and Johnstown, a handsome son of Man o' War galloped to great acclaim at Belmont Park. War Admiral, like his sire, was owned by textile merchant Samuel D. Riddle. However, unlike the strapping Big Red, the "Admiral" was smallish in stature, with a shiny, seal brown coat that often appeared black. He did, however, possess the excitable temperament that had passed through the Fair Play line. War Admiral was regarded by his riders as difficult to handle, and he showed an aversion to the starting gate, which often delayed the start of his races by several minutes. Once loaded, however, he took command of the track.

Starting gates, or stall machines, were in common use at this time at Belmont Park, as well as at other area racetracks. In the mid-1930s, Joseph Widener had tested an Australian starting gate at Belmont, which was later investigated and replaced due to what the *New York Times* described as "dissatisfaction by owners." In 1936, Widener tested a newer version of the gate at Hialeah before implementing it at Belmont. Prior to the use of starting gates, horses were sent off in races using various web and rope barriers. Horses were lined up facing away from the barrier and were turned around at the start of the race. These methods often resulted in premature starts and jockey errors and, according to some sources, resulted in Man o' War's only career loss. The first electric starting gate would be implemented in 1940.

Despite War Admiral's dislike for the starting gate, he proved himself a force to be reckoned with on the track. He began his three-year-old season

War Admiral, 1937 Triple Crown champion. *Library of Congress photo.*

with a romp in a six-furlong overnight race at Havre de Grace. Then, despite a seven-minute delay due to his starting gate issues, led wire-to-wire in a six-length victory in the Chesapeake Stakes. After a similar eight-minute delay in the Kentucky Derby, the gallant colt led wire-to-wire in winning the 1937 Run for the Roses. He capped off that win with a hard-fought victory in the Preakness, in which he outdueled juvenile champion Pompoon in a thrilling stretch drive.

If spectators were still unsure of his mettle, War Admiral proved it in the Belmont Stakes. The seal brown colt stumbled at the start of the race, catching and damaging a portion of his right rear hoof. The champion's heart prevailed over the injury, and he led wire-to-wire in carrying Riddle's black-and-gold racing silks to Triple Crown glory. In the process, the Admiral tied the American record of 2:28:60 for a mile and a half. He was unbeaten in eight starts that season, earning Horse of the Year honors. War Admiral's success would continue in the following year; his wins included a three-length victory in the Jockey Club Gold Cup over two miles at Belmont Park.

Notwithstanding his many achievements, War Admiral became best remembered, perhaps, for a race that he did not win. In 1938, the Admiral was bested by four lengths by Charles Howard's Seabiscuit in a much-publicized match race at Pimlico Race Course. (The race had originally been scheduled to be held at Belmont Park.) Nevertheless, War Admiral remains one of Belmont Park's—and racing's—greatest champions. Following his retirement to stud in 1939, his bloodlines would live on in some of racing's later immortals, including his daughter Busanda, dam of the 1966 Horse of the Year, Buckpasser.

In the year following War Admiral's victory in the Gold Cup, a new president was appointed at Belmont Park. Prominent horseman Alfred Gwynne Vanderbilt, at twenty-seven years of age, succeeded the aging Joseph Widener. Vanderbilt served simultaneously as president of Pimlico Racecourse, a position he had held since the age of twenty, and had, in fact, arranged the match race between Seabiscuit and War Admiral. In 1935, Vanderbilt was the youngest member in the history of the Jockey Club. He was also the owner of Sagamore Farm in Maryland, whose string of champions would include the great handicap horse Discovery and, later, the immortal Native Dancer.

The onset of World War II would dramatically impact American spending, but the start of the war did little to dim the spirits of racing enthusiasts at Belmont Park. The year 1941 witnessed the prominence of the colt Whirlaway and marked the beginning of the Calumet Farm racing dynasty. The Lexington, Kentucky–based farm would dominate the sport over the next two decades, with two Triple Crown winners and numerous wins at Belmont Park. Calumet would also hold the distinction as the leading money-winning farm for an unprecedented period of twelve years.

Calumet Farm had been established in 1924 by William Monroe Wright, owner and founder of the Calumet Baking Powder Company. Wright had his first taste of success at Belmont Park when his horse Hadagal won the 1933 Champagne Stakes. From that time forward, Calumet's brightly colored "devil red" and blue silks would prove a frequent sight in the Belmont winner's circle.

Whirlaway, a stunning chestnut son of Epsom Derby winner Blenheim II, was one of Calumet's greatest champions. The colt was from Blenheim II's first U.S. crop and was known affectionately as "Mr. Longtail" due to

Whirlaway, 1941 Triple Crown champion. *Library of Congress photo.*

his lush, flowing tail. Whirlaway was trained by Ben A. Jones and ridden by the great Eddie Arcaro during his three-year-old season. Despite possessing great talent, the colt was known for his difficulty, being prone to drifting, or "bearing out," to the middle of the track. This had resulted in several losses, frustrating Jones, who referred to the colt as "the half wit." In the 1940 Saratoga Special, Whirlaway drifted so far as to actually crash into the rail before catching himself and ultimately winning the race.

In preparation for the Kentucky Derby, Jones created a special blinker that included a cup only on the right eye, thereby holding the colt's focus and enabling Arcaro to more easily guide him. On the day of the race, the trainer cut a small hole in the blinker cup, allowing for a small field of vision. The unconventional plan worked, as Whirlaway won the Derby by eight lengths, setting a time record in the process. He went on to win the Preakness before heading to Belmont Park, where he dominated over a fast track before a crowd of 30,081. The *New York Times* wrote: "The chestnut colt from the Calumet Farm raced through the stretch so easily that he had his ears pricking, and he also had that mightiest Triple Crown tilted jauntily on his handsome forelock. When he finished the historic mile and a half run that grossed $52,270 in 2:31 flat over a fast track, the son of Blenheim II and Dustwhirl became the fifth horse in American racing history to capture the Kentucky Derby, Preakness and Belmont Stakes."[20]

Whirlaway's success would continue as a four-year-old; his wins that year included the Jockey Club Gold Cup over two miles at Belmont Park.

While many racetracks had been closed down during the wartime years, Belmont Park remained open. In 1940, the racetrack hosted "War Relief Day," with proceeds benefiting the American Red Cross. In 1942, Belmont Park contributed to war relief efforts with an extra seven days of racing during the season. The *New York Times* noted that "there were enough competitive thrills to content the most exacting during the racing season, but as the year drew to a close thoroughbred followers paid more attention to how the sport had got along under war conditions. The raising of approximately $3,000,000 for service men, with the biggest single contribution coming from seven extra days at Belmont Park, was merely one phase of dovetailing racing with the war effort."[21] In 1943, the racetrack hosted "Back the Attack" Day, in which a war bond purchase was required to gain admission to Belmont Park. According to the New York Racing Association, total receipts for Back the Attack Day were estimated at between $25 and $30 million.

In 1943, racing fans were treated to yet another Triple Crown triumph with the victory of the colt Count Fleet. A son of Belmont winner Reigh Count, Count Fleet was also owned by John D. Hertz, founder of the Yellow Cab Company. As a foal, Count Fleet had proven difficult to handle, and Hertz decided to offer him for sale. The horse's misbehavior discouraged all potential buyers, however, and Hertz was forced to keep him. Hertz again tried to sell the horse as a two-year-old, following disappointing efforts in his first two starts. However, Hertz's stable hand Sam Ramsen and jockey Johnny Longden saw promise in the colt and pleaded with Hertz to reconsider. It proved to be a wise decision, as the colt broke his maiden shortly thereafter and then galloped to victory in the Champagne Stakes. He began his three-year-old season with wins in the St. James Purse and the Wood Memorial, despite injuring his left hind leg in the latter. The colt quickly recovered, winning the Kentucky Derby by three lengths and capping it off with a victory in the Preakness. At Belmont Park, he romped to what the *New York Times* called "a 30-length waltz," becoming America's sixth Triple Crown winner. Count Fleet retired after his three-year-old season, owing to a reinjuring of his right hind leg.

Count Fleet, winner of the Triple Crown in 1943. *Library of Congress photo.*

In the year following the coronation of Count Fleet, spectators witnessed the first Triple Crown "near miss" when Kentucky Derby and Preakness winner Pensive was narrowly defeated in the Belmont Stakes. Calumet Farm's Pensive was a son of the British stallion Hyperion, winner of England's Epsom Derby and St. Leger Stakes.

After handily winning the Kentucky Derby and Preakness Stakes, Pensive seemed poised to bring another Triple Crown to Calumet Farm. For the occasion, the Belmont purse had been increased to $50,000, and crowds swarmed the racetrack to witness history in the making. The *New York Times* wrote, "Pensive's 'great day' is finally at hand—the day when a question racegoers have asked time and again after his memorable triumph in the Kentucky Derby finally will be answered."[22]

It appeared on Belmont Stakes day that the crown was Pensive's to lose, and he was sent off as the betting line favorite. After leading until the last quarter mile, the colt was narrowly upset by William Zeigler's aptly named horse, Bounding Home. Following this loss, Pensive would fail to win any other race, despite completing eight starts. He was retired to stud duty, where he would sire the colt Ponder, winner of the 1949 Kentucky Derby and Jockey Club Gold Cup.

Around the time of Pensive's stunning loss at Belmont, wartime relief efforts continued at the racetrack, and significant monies were raised for charity. Additionally, government-ordered travel restrictions prohibited the transport of horses via rail, and Saratoga Race Course was closed from 1943 to 1945. Racing was moved to Belmont Park for all three seasons before returning to the Spa for the 1946 season. That year, spectators at Belmont Park celebrated the Triple Crown victory of Assault, a son of Kentucky Derby and Preakness winner Bold Venture. Despite this lineage, Assault was an unlikely champion, as he walked with a limp, the result of an injury sustained as a young colt. However, the injury did little to discourage the colt from galloping, and his speed, coupled with his unique way of moving, earned him the nickname the "Club-Footed Comet." Assault was foaled at King Ranch, a farm in Texas that primarily raised quarter horses and cattle rather than champion Thoroughbreds.

As a two-year-old, Assault had won only two of nine races. He rebounded at the start of his three-year-old season with a win in the Wood Memorial before a falter in the Derby Trial appeared to lessen his chances for victory on the first Saturday in May. The colt defied the odds, however, winning the Derby by an astounding eight lengths—the largest margin of victory at that time.

Fresh off the Derby victory, Assault became the favorite for the Preakness Stakes. After being boxed in early in the race, the colt opened up a four-length lead with a furlong remaining. Tiring in the stretch, he was challenged by Lord Boswell but ultimately claimed the Preakness by a neck. It was then off to Belmont Park for the true test of the colt's mettle. Bettors, questioning Assault's ability to tackle the grueling one and a half miles, favored Lord Boswell in the Belmont Stakes. For much of the race, it appeared that the bettors were going to be correct, as Assault stumbled out of the gate and trailed the field by a considerable margin. The Club Footed Comet made his move in the final two hundred yards, ultimately winning the Belmont by three lengths and becoming America's seventh Triple Crown champion.

The following season, Assault won five of his seven starts, which included both the Brooklyn and Suburban Handicaps. On September 27, 1947, the grandstand at Belmont was filled to capacity as Assault, ridden by Eddie Arcaro, faced the Calumet colt Armed in a $100,000 winner-take-all match race over Big Sandy. According to some sources, Assault had shown some lameness in the days leading up to race and was therefore not at his best. Armed bested Assault by a full eight lengths, earning the winner's purse as well as seasonal Horse of the

Assault, 1946 Triple Crown champion. *Library of Congress photo.*

Year honors. After proving sterile at stud, Assault went on to race until the age of seven before ultimately being retired at King Ranch.

Calumet Farm's success continued in 1948 with the Triple Crown victory of the colt Citation. A son of the great Bull Lea, "Big Cy" showed championship form in his two-year-old season with only a single loss, to his stablemate, Bewitch (also sired by Bull Lea). Citation began his three-year-old campaign with victories over older horses, including the aforementioned Armed, in the Groundhog Purse and Seminole Stakes at Hialeah. On the heels of these victories, Big Cy captured both the Everglades and the Flamingo Stakes. Tragedy struck, however, when the colt's regular jockey, Albert "Al" Snider, drowned while fishing in Florida. Snider was replaced by the great Eddie Arcaro, whose resumé at that point included three Kentucky Derby wins.

With Arcaro in the irons, Citation would defeat his Calumet stablemate, Coaltown, by three and a half lengths to win the Run for the Roses. (According to sources, Arcaro presented a share of his Derby purse to the widow of former jockey Al Snider.) Citation continued his winning ways with a five-and-a-half-length victory in the Preakness. At Belmont, Citation

Citation, winner of the 1948 Triple Crown. *Library of Congress photo.*

tied the stakes record of 2:28:20 previously set by Count Fleet and became the eighth American Triple Crown champion.

Following this victory, Big Cy tied the track record set by Armed in the Stars and Stripes Handicap at Arlington Park and cruised to victory in both the American Derby and the Sysonby Mile. Returning to Belmont, Citation dominated the two-mile Jockey Club Gold Cup, defeating 1947 Preakness champion Phalynx by a full seven lengths. By the end of the season, Citation had amassed nineteen wins in twenty starts and set a new single season earnings record. In Horse of the Year voting conducted by *Turf and Sport Digest* magazine, Citation gained 161 of a possible 163 votes. In 1951, Big Cy became the first racehorse in history to earn a record $1 million.

The 1940s proved to be one of the most successful decades in racing, with the Triple Crown coronations of Whirlaway, Count Fleet, Assault and Citation. These superstars would draw legions of new fans to the sport as the "decade of champions" came to a close. By 1950, the times were changing with the arrival of the age of television, and its effects would be felt at Belmont Park in the years to come.

Chapter 11

THE MODERN AGE

The 1950s brought a new element to horse racing with the advent of the age of television. Key races could now be shown on TV, introducing the sport to a larger audience. Television created an array of new celebrities, and not all were of the human variety. One of the most popular stars of the early 1950s, and a frequent presence at Belmont Park, was Alfred Vanderbilt's Native Dancer. Known as the "Grey Ghost" due to his dazzling color, Native Dancer left a lasting impression on New York racing. In 1952, as a two-year-old, he captured a series of important races in his trademark dramatic come-from-behind style. Undefeated as a juvenile, Native Dancer set a world record of 1:14:40 for six and a half furlongs in the Futurity at Belmont and became the first two-year-old to be named Horse of the Year. Trainer Bill Winfrey told the media, "The gray is the fastest horse I've ever trained. He shows good times in workouts, but that's not what's impressive. It's the fact that the big gray does it without any effort. He actually seems to be holding himself back."[23]

Native Dancer's stunning color, which was illuminated against the field of common chestnuts, blacks and bays, made him a perfect subject for television. The Grey Ghost became an instant hero in the weeks leading up to the Triple Crown races. As his fan base grew, the horse's every move was followed by the media, and his major races were aired on TV. A survey by the magazine *TV Guide* noted that Native Dancer's popularity at that time was second only to entertainer Ed Sullivan as "the biggest attraction on television."

Native Dancer, the "Grey Ghost." *Photo courtesy Keeneland Library.*

In 1953, after losing the Kentucky Derby to the long shot Dark Star, Native Dancer won both the Preakness and the Belmont Stakes by a neck. His time of 2:28:60 for the mile and a half in the Belmont was just short of the speed records posted by the great Citation and Count Fleet. The following year, his wins would include the Met Mile, which he captured by a neck over Straight Face after lagging seven lengths behind, carrying 130 pounds to Straight Face's 117. Native Dancer became the third horse (besides Duke of Magenta and Man o' War) to win the Preakness, Belmont and Travers in conjunction with the Withers Stakes.

One of Native Dancer's top rivals was Tom Fool, a strapping bay colt owned by the Whitneys' Greentree Stable. Foaled one year prior to Native Dancer, Tom Fool had won five of seven starts in his two-year-old season, placing second in his remaining races and earning champion two-year-old colt honors. After placing second in the Wood Memorial at Jamaica as a three-year-old, the colt developed a high fever that would keep him out of the Triple Crown races. He returned, ready for battle, as a four-year-old in 1953, winning a series of ten consecutive races and becoming only the second horse in history to win New York's Handicap Triple Crown. Based on that record, Tom Fool edged out Native Dancer for 1953 Horse of the Year honors, with the Grey Ghost earning back the title the following year.

The appearance of these two outstanding horses brought Thoroughbred racing to a new level. Many hoped that the two would face off on the racetrack; however, a recurring injury to Native Dancer's foot made such a meeting impossible. Tom Fool was retired to stud at the end of 1953 while Native Dancer raced for one more season. Both colts went on to successful careers in the breeding shed, siring a number of prominent stakes winners. Tom Fool's progeny included 1958 Kentucky Derby and Preakness winner Tim Tam and the aforementioned Buckpasser. Native Dancer's offspring included Kauai King, which avenged his sire's one loss with a victory in the 1966 Kentucky Derby.

As Native Dancer and Tom Fool respectively made their way to the breeding shed, another superstar colt appeared on the scene. The bay colt Nashua, a son of the temperamental but speedy Nasrullah, arrived at Belmont Park as a two-year-old under the guidance of trainer Sunny Jim Fitzsimmons. Nashua was bred by Belair Stud's William Woodward Sr., whose intentions had been to race the colt in the Epsom Derby in England. Sadly, Woodward died when the colt was still a yearling. Woodward's son, William Jr. (aka "Billy"), the new master of Belair Stud, assumed ownership of the horse and opted to race him in the United States.

Tom Fool, winner of the New York Handicap Triple Crown. *Photo courtesy Keeneland Library.*

Nashua with owner Billy Woodward and jockey Eddie Arcaro. *Photo courtesy Belair Stable Museum.*

Nashua made his racing debut on May 5, 1954, at Belmont Park over a distance of four and a half furlongs. In a field of twenty-one maidens, the attractive bay colt showed impressive form. Nashua broke from post position fourteen, with Fitzsimmons's regular rider Jess Higley perched squarely in the saddle. Nashua, which Fitzsimmons had nicknamed "Mickey" due to his Irish heritage, ran effortlessly, besting the field by three lengths in a time of 0:52:60. In the starting gate next to Nashua was the colt Golden Prince, ridden by none other than Eddie Arcaro. Gifted with a keen eye and intelligence beyond his years, Arcaro saw early brilliance in Nashua on that day at Big Sandy. He later told *Sports Illustrated*:

> *The first time I saw Nashua—or at least the first time I can remember seeing him—I had better than a clubhouse seat. The occasion was a four-and-a-half furlong maiden race at Belmont Park almost exactly a year ago, on May 5, 1954. I was on Mrs. L. Lazare's Golden Prince, breaking from post position 13. Next to me in 14 was Jess Higley on Nashua. During the*

race I had problems enough of my own, but I still have a vivid recollection of Nashua turning on a wonderful burst of speed and winning easily by three lengths. My horse finished 11th.

Sometimes a jockey can see qualities in a horse that make him immediately want to ride that horse in future races. I have had such a "second sense" about horses before this—with Assault and Citation, for instance. In Nashua's case I knew instinctively as he drew away from his field that this was a horse with a determined will to win.[24]

After the race, Arcaro approached Fitzsimmons to inquire about the prospect of gaining the mount on Nashua. A deal was made, and a great partnership commenced. Arcaro's first race aboard the strapping bay came just one short week after Nashua's debut. In the five-furlong Juvenile Stakes at Belmont, Nashua would face the horse that was to become his primary rival. Summer Tan, a precocious colt owned by Dorothy Firestone, was to challenge Nashua on various occasions. However, Nashua took top honors in this first meeting of the two, besting his new rival in a one-and-a-half-length win.

Sunny Jim was known for racing his horses frequently, and Nashua's schedule was no different. One week after the Juvenile Stakes, Nashua headed to New Jersey for the five-furlong Cherry Hill Stakes at Garden State. As Arcaro was serving a brief suspension, Jess Higley returned for the ride on Nashua. Despite urging from Higley, Nashua lost by a head to Royal Note while closing five lengths ahead of the third-place finisher.

On the heels of this defeat, Nashua headed back to Belmont for the six-furlong Anticipation Purse, which was to serve as the colt's prep for the upcoming Futurity. Nashua proved he was ready for the challenge and did so impressively, winning by a length over Royal Coinage and equaling the existing track record of 1:08.20. This victory solidified Nashua's status as the favorite for the Futurity, and he would carry high weight of 122 pounds. As expected, the Futurity came down to a thrilling duel between Nashua and Summer Tan, with Nashua ultimately winning by a head. As this was the first Futurity victory for the legendary Jim Fitzsimmons, a special trophy was created commemorating the event.

Nashua raced eight times as a juvenile, amassing six wins and two second-place finishes, which earned him champion two-year-old colt honors. After a four-month layoff in which Nashua grew in height and girth, the horse began his three-year-old season by winning a series of Derby prep races in Florida. He capped off his position as the Derby favorite with a defeat of rival Summer Tan in the Wood Memorial. At Churchill Downs, however, Nashua was upset by

THE BELMONT
BELMONT PARK .. $100,000 ADDED .. JUNE 11, 1955
BELAIR STUD'S NASHUA EDDIE ARCARO up
J. FITZSIMMONS trainer 1112 Miles Time 2:29
BLAZING COUNT 2nd PORTERSVILLE 3rd
Presentation By The Hon. H.E. Talbott

Nashua wins the 1955 Belmont Stakes. *Photo courtesy Belair Stable Museum.*

West Coast favorite Swaps, ridden by the young and talented Willie Shoemaker. Both Arcaro and Fitzsimmons blamed themselves for the loss, noting that they had been too focused on Summer Tan to take note of the fast-running Swaps.

Following the Derby, Swaps returned to the West Coast, leaving Nashua to dominate the Preakness Stakes. He won in a record time of 1:54:30 before heading to Belmont. The race over Big Sandy was all Nashua, and the colt dominated the rest of the field by an electrifying nine lengths, bringing a sixth Belmont Stakes trophy to Belair Stud. Nashua's winning ways continued in the Dwyer Stakes and the Arlington Classic. The Belair colt then avenged his Kentucky Derby loss by defeating his rival Swaps in a much-heralded match race at Chicago's Arlington Park.

Three weeks after the match race, Nashua took on older horses in the Sysonby Stakes at Belmont, where he placed a disappointing third behind the elder High Gun. The race had added a $100,000 purse with the hope of attracting both Swaps and Nashua, but Swaps was nursing an old hoof problem that he had allegedly reinjured in the match race. Nashua completed his classic season at none other than Belmont Park with a win in the Jockey Club Gold Cup over two miles. The Belair Stud champion was subsequently named 1955 Horse of the Year.

Outside the racetrack, Nashua's story would gain additional media coverage when, in an odd twist of fate, William Woodward Jr. was shot to death in his home on October 30, 1955. The young master of Belair was killed by his own wife, Ann, who claimed to have mistaken her husband for an

Owner Billy Woodward (second from right) accepts the August Belmont Trophy for Nashua's Belmont Stakes win. *Photo courtesy Belair Stable Museum.*

intruder. Woodward's death made worldwide headlines, with *Life* magazine referring to it as the "Shooting of the Century," spurring storylines for novels by acclaimed writers Truman Capote and Dominick Dunne.

In the aftermath of Billy Woodward's death, Nashua was sold in a sealed-bid auction. He became the first racehorse to be sold for over $1 million when he was purchased by a syndicate led by Leslie Combs II of Spendthrift Farm. Nashua retired to stud in 1956, having surpassed the earnings record previously set by Triple Crown champion Citation. His wins as a four-year-old included a second consecutive Jockey Club Gold Cup at Belmont Park; this feat would later be duplicated by one of his offspring, the filly Shuvee, which would capture consecutive runnings of the race in 1970 and 1971.

Meanwhile, the structure of Belmont management changed when state legislators determined that a nonprofit association should be formed to oversee New York racing in an attempt to revitalize the sport. This resulted in the formation of the Greater New York Association (GNYA). In 1955, shareholders of the four New York racetracks operating at that time

(Belmont, Saratoga, Jamaica and Aqueduct) sold out to the GNYA, with Belmont shares purchased at a cost of ninety-one dollars each. The GNYA was later renamed the New York Racing Association (NYRA). One of its original founders was Christopher T. Chenery, who would later become known as the breeder of Secretariat.

After much planning and consideration, the NYRA decided that Belmont Park, along with Aqueduct and Saratoga, would be renovated while the Jamaica racecourse would permanently be closed. It was determined that Aqueduct would be the first of the three to be reconstructed, owing to its proximity to the New York subway system. The new Aqueduct, known as the "Big A," would be reopened in 1959 while Belmont would undergo a renovation in the early to mid-1960s. During this period, some of the larger races on the Belmont card would be moved to the new "Big A."

In the meantime, during the renovation of Aqueduct, racing continued in all its splendor at the aging Belmont Park. In 1958, Calumet Farm hovered on the verge of a third Triple Crown when its favored colt, Tim Tam, entered the Belmont Stakes as the favorite. A son of Tom Fool, the dark bay colt had handily captured both the Kentucky Derby and Preakness Stakes and appeared poised for victory over the Belmont dirt track. Unfortunately, the colt sustained a career-ending fracture of a sesamoid bone in his right foreleg and was unable to retain the lead to the finish. The race was won by the sturdy Irish-bred Cavan, with Tim Tam placing a gallant second. *Sports Illustrated* would later write: "This 90th Belmont Stakes will be forever remembered as having been won by a promising fine-looking newcomer and yet lost by a colt who seemed destined from birth for greatness."[25] In an odd twist of fate, Cavan himself would sustain a career-ending injury in his next start, the Peter Pan Stakes, named in honor of the 1907 Belmont Stakes winner.

At the emergence of the new decade, spectators at Belmont Park were introduced to the greatness of the gelding Kelso, which would win an unprecedented five consecutive occurrences of the Jockey Club Gold Cup. Among the horse's other triumphs were three runnings each of the Woodward and Whitney Stakes. However, as New York racing was in transition during this time, many of Kelso's races took place at Aqueduct rather than Belmont Park. Kelso's first win at Belmont was the 1960 Lawrence Realization, where he matched the track record of 2:40:80 over one and five-eighths miles, which had been previously set by the immortal Man o' War. The following year, Kelso became the third horse (behind Whisk Broom II and Tom Fool) to win the New York Handicap Triple Crown, with all three races held at Aqueduct that season.

The great Kelso is led into the Belmont paddock in 1961, with jockey Eddie Arcaro and trainer Carl Hanford. *Photo courtesy Keeneland Library.*

The speedy Kelso, known as "King Kelly" to his fans, returned to Belmont for the running of the 1961 Whitney Stakes, which had been moved for the short term from Saratoga Race Course. That season, Kelso also won the Woodward at Belmont, matching the track record for ten furlongs that had been set by Whisk Broom II in the 1913 Suburban. Trainer Carl Hanford later said of the gelding, "He was an extremely determined horse. If he saw a horse in front, he wanted to get to him. You could take him back or send him to the front. He was an extremely sound horse who was light on his feet with incredible balance. Kelso could wheel on a dime, spinning round in a circle and never letting his feet touch each other."[26]

Kelso retired from racing in 1966 at the age of nine, having won an unparalleled five Horse of the Year titles. He subsequently enjoyed a second career as a show jumper and foxhunter for owner Allaire DuPont. Kelso visited Belmont Park for the very last time on October 15, 1983. Prior to the start of the Jockey Club Gold Cup, the twenty-six-year-old Kelso paraded, along with two other outstanding geldings, Forego and John Henry, before

Beautiful Belmont Park. *Photo courtesy Jason Moran.*

A view of the grandstand. *Photo courtesy Cindy Dulay, horse-races.net.*

The paddock. *Photo courtesy Cindy Dulay, horse-races.net.*

View of the winner's circle. *Photo courtesy Jason Moran.*

A view of "Big Sandy." *Photo courtesy Cindy Dulay, horse-races.net.*

The NYPD mounted unit at the Belmont Stakes. *Photo courtesy Cindy Dulay, horse-races.net.*

The grandstand. *Photo courtesy Cindy Dulay, horse-races.net.*

The bugler entertains the crowd. *Photo courtesy Allison Pareis.*

Opposite, top: Back to the barn. *Photo courtesy Jessie Holmes.*

Opposite, bottom: The legendary Secretariat. *Photo courtesy Bob Coglianese.*

The Secretariat statue on Belmont Stakes day. *Photo courtesy Allison Pareis.*

The beautiful and talented Ruffian. *Photo courtesy Bob Coglianese.*

A horse gallops in front of Ruffian's grave. *Photo courtesy Jason Moran.*

Seattle Slew wins the 1978 Marlboro Cup. *Photo courtesy Adam Coglianese.*

Swale in the 1984 Belmont Stakes winner's circle. *Photo courtesy Bud Morton.*

Victory Gallop defeats Real Quiet in the 1998 Belmont Stakes. *Photo courtesy Bud Morton.*

Sarava wins the 2002 Belmont Stakes. *Photo courtesy Bud Morton.*

Birdstone defeats Smarty Jones in the 2004 Belmont Stakes. *Photo courtesy Bud Morton.*

Bernardini wins the 2006 Jockey Club Gold Cup. *Photo courtesy Cindy Dulay, horse-races.net.*

Opposite, top: Rags to Riches defeats Curlin in the 2007 Belmont Stakes. *Photo courtesy Cindy Dulay, horse-races.net.*

Opposite, bottom: Curlin, two-time winner of the Jockey Club Gold Cup. *Photo courtesy Cindy Dulay, horse-races.net.*

Big Brown is pulled up in the 2008 Belmont Stakes. *Photo courtesy Allison Pareis.*

Da Tara upsets Big Brown's bid for the 2008 Triple Crown. *Photo courtesy Allison Pareis.*

Rachel Alexandra, winner of the 2009 Mother Goose Stakes. *Photo courtesy Jessie Holmes.*

Summer Bird wins the 2009 Belmont Stakes. *Photo courtesy Cindy Dulay, horse-races.net.*

Haynesfield wins the 2010 Jockey Club Gold Cup. *Photo courtesy Cindy Dulay, horse-races.net.*

Drosselmeyer wins the 2010 Belmont Stakes. *Photo courtesy Jessie Holmes.*

Opposite, bottom: I'll Have Another's retirement ceremony. *Photo courtesy Jason Moran.*

Above, left: Ruler on Ice, winner of the 2011 Belmont Stakes. *Photo courtesy Jessie Holmes.*

Above, right: Flat Out, two-time winner of the Jockey Club Gold Cup. *Photo courtesy Jessie Holmes.*

Union Rags works at Belmont Park. *Photo courtesy Jessie Holmes.*

Union Rags defeats Paynter in the 2012 Belmont Stakes. *Photo courtesy Cindy Dulay, horse-races.net.*

a crowd of thirty-two thousand spectators. It was to be Kelso's final adieu, as the gelding died of colic the very next day. He was buried in the equine cemetery at his owner's Woodstock Farm in Chesapeake City, Maryland.

While Kelso was setting various records in the 1962 season, Belmont Park was razed for its reconstruction and would be closed for five years. According to author Edward Bowen, "Arthur Froehlich's design duplicated the red brick and sandstone of the old Belmont and emphasized handsome arched windows."[27] The paddock area and its adornments were preserved, but the old Manice mansion was replaced with a more modernized clubhouse. The reconstruction of Belmont Park was completed at an estimated cost of $31 million. The "new" Belmont Park opened on May 20, 1968, with a grandstand that, when measured in length, is larger than the Empire State Building.

The first Belmont Stakes held at the reconstructed facility was won by Stage Door Johnny, a chestnut colt owned by John Hay Whitney of the prominent Whitney family. In winning the Belmont, the horse deprived Calumet Farm of winning a sought-after third Triple Crown. However, had Calumet's colt, Forward Pass, won the Belmont Stakes, there would likely have been some questions raised by fans of the sport. While Forward Pass had handily won the Preakness Stakes, he had actually finished second in the Run for the Roses. Forward Pass had been named the winner of the Kentucky Derby only after the disqualification of another colt, Dancer's Image, who was found to have traces of a forbidden substance in his system.

By the turn of the decade, the American racing public was desperately hoping for another Triple Crown winner. One year after the defeat of Forward Pass, spectators at Belmont Park witnessed yet another near miss. This time it was the then-undefeated colt Majestic Prince that was denied Triple Crown glory. The bright chestnut colt was beaten squarely by Arts and Letters, a horse owned by the noted philanthropist Paul Mellon.

Mellon's colt had proven a formidable opponent for Majestic Prince, which had won both the Derby and Preakness by the narrowest of margins. The "Prince" had bested Arts and Letters by a neck in the Derby and topped the Mellon colt by a mere head in the Preakness. Following the Preakness win, trainer (and well-known former jockey) Johnny Longden told the media that Majestic Prince was suffering from tendon soreness and would thus be absent from the Belmont Stakes. As there was no apparent outward evidence of this injury, Longden's words sent the media into an utter frenzy. Many felt that the colt was indeed fit to run and that Longden simply feared that the colt would be beaten at Belmont. In response, *Sports Illustrated* boasted a headline that read, "The Prince Ducks the Big One."

Such pressures from the media troubled the horse's owner, Frank McMahon, who likely wanted his own shot at racing immortality. Therefore, despite Longden's recommendation that Majestic Prince return home to California, McMahon opted to send his colt to New York to prepare for the Belmont Stakes. According to sources, this resulted in a shouting match between Longden and McMahon a few days prior to the race. Nevertheless, Majestic Prince was entered in the Belmont Stakes, where he finished a disappointing five and a half lengths behind Arts and Letters. Majestic Prince would never race again; after attempting two comebacks in the following years, the gallant colt was retired to stud. His progeny would include Coastal, winner of the 1979 Belmont Stakes.

For his part, Arts and Letters enjoyed a thoroughly successful racing career. After his Belmont Stakes victory, the colt went on to win several noted stakes races, including the Travers, Met Mile, Jockey Club Gold Cup and Woodward Stakes. His offspring would include the gelding Winters Tale, winner of the Marlboro Cup, Brooklyn Handicap and Suburban Handicap races.

In 1971, the Belmont Stakes attracted a record crowd as another champion attempted to win the seemingly elusive Triple Crown. Canonero II, winner of the Derby and Preakness that year, originally had appeared to be an unlikely candidate. Bred in the United States, the colt's noticeably crooked front leg had resulted in the estimation that he had no future as a racehorse. However, Venezuelan Edgar Caibett noticed something special about the colt and purchased him for the meager sum of $1,200.

After a less than stellar juvenile season in Venezuela, the colt was shipped to the United States for the Kentucky Derby. Dismissed by both the media and the betting public, Canonero II went on to win the Derby by three and three-quarters lengths. With his Derby victory attributed to a "fluke," Canonero II proved the experts wrong as he cruised to victory in the Preakness Stakes at Pimlico.

Similar to the seven would-be champions that had come before him, Canonero II was unable to live up to the challenge posed by the grueling Belmont Stakes, and the horse crossed the finish line in fourth place. Many attributed this poor showing to a hoof infection that had plagued the colt in the days leading up to the race. While he was unsuccessful in winning the Belmont Stakes, Canonero II would make his own mark at Belmont Park the following year, setting a track record in the Stymie Handicap over a mile and a furlong while defeating the reigning Derby and Belmont champion Riva Ridge. In the words of Pimlico general manager Chick Lang, "It was like Disneyland to be around Canonero II. It was thrilling."[28]

Chapter 12

TRIUMPH AND TRAGEDY

By the early 1970s, fans of American horse racing were eager for a new Triple Crown winner. Since Citation's victory in 1948, no horse had won the trio of races. Fans of the sport, questioning whether there would ever be a successor to Citation, eagerly awaited the coronation of the newest Triple Crown champion.

In 1972, Riva Ridge won the Belmont Stakes in commanding fashion. While the colt had won the Kentucky Derby, he faltered in the subsequent Preakness, thereby losing any chance of a Triple Crown before even heading to Belmont.

A plain bay with a kind face and droopy ears, Riva Ridge was the entry of the Virginia-based Meadow Stables. Christopher Chenery, one of the original founders of the NYRA, established the farm in 1932 and raised Thoroughbreds under the Meadow Stud banner. The farm had produced several champions, including 1950 Horse of the Year Hill Prince; Cicada, the first filly to win championship honors as a two-, three- and four-year-old; and First Landing, champion two-year-old colt in 1958. Riva Ridge, a son of First Landing, was named in honor of Chenery's son-in-law, John Tweedy, who had been a part of a U.S. victory at Riva Ridge in Italy in World War II.

In the early 1970s, as Chris Chenery was in failing health, the operation of Meadow Stables fell to his daughter, Helen "Penny" Tweedy. Penny also oversaw the farm's breeding stock, which included a bright chestnut foal by the name of Secretariat. With near-perfect conformation and the striking looks of a matinee idol, the two-year-old Secretariat commanded attention when he first set foot on Belmont's historic grounds. Even his nickname evoked greatness; like the immortal Man o' War, the chestnut colt was affectionately called "Big Red."

Secretariat would be entered in the Belmont Futurity on September 16, 1972, after a series of four consecutive victories that included Saratoga's Sanford and Hopeful Stakes. The brawny, red colt took easily to the Belmont dirt track, winning the Futurity by one and three-quarters lengths over Stop the Music and earning his largest purse to date of $80,000. At the end of the season, Secretariat was not only named champion two-year-old colt but also the overall Horse of the Year.

Secretariat's popularity increased tremendously the following spring when he handily won the Kentucky Derby and Preakness, setting new track records and pinning the public's hopes on the ever-elusive Triple Crown. The early 1970s was a time of unrest in America, and the red horse fulfilled the country's need for a hero. When Secretariat arrived at Belmont Park in early June, the media trailed the big colt's every move; a true celebrity, he had appeared on the covers of *Time*, *Newsweek* and *Sports Illustrated*.

In the days leading up to the Belmont Stakes, Secretariat impressed the crowds with his pre-race workouts. On June 2, 1973, the *New York Times* heralded, "Secretariat Fast Even in Practice." The colt posted a workout over one mile on the dirt in 1:34:80, which matched the time that had been set by Linda's Chief in winning the Withers Mile just days earlier.

Despite Secretariat's impressive workouts, it is unlikely that anyone expected the display of raw power that the colt would unleash in the Belmont Stakes. On June 9, 1973, Secretariat dominated the field of four horses, which included Derby and Preakness runner-up Sham. Breaking from the outside, Secretariat dazzled the crowd of 67,605 from start to finish as he and Sham opened an early lead of ten lengths over the rest of the field. While Sham began to tire after six furlongs, Secretariat appeared to gain momentum with each passing stride. In what was to become the most famous of race calls, Chic Anderson announced, "Secretariat is moving like a tremendous machine!"

Secretariat's Belmont performance, in which he bested his closest rival by an astounding thirty-one lengths in record time, set a standard that is yet to be matched. The *New York Times* wrote:

> *Secretariat won the Belmont Stakes yesterday with a finality that was incredible. The Meadow Stable star flashed to success in the 1½-mile event by the improbable margin of 31 lengths over Twice a Prince, his runner-up, and, even with the big margin, he set a track record time of 2:24.*[29]

A new king had been crowned. Secretariat's Belmont Stakes performance is widely regarded as one of the greatest moments in the history of all sports.

While Secretariat remains one of the greatest equine athletes of all time, the colt was not invincible. After handily winning the Arlington Invitational in late June, Secretariat was upset by the Allen Jerkens–trained Onion in the Whitney at Saratoga. Following this race, Onion's trainer, Allan Jerkens, would be nicknamed the "Giant Killer," due to his apparent knack for defeating odds-on favorites. One month after the Whitney, Jerkens would get the best of Secretariat once more, when his sixteen-to-one entry, Prove Out, conquered Big Red in the Woodward Stakes at Belmont Park.

That summer, there had been plans to organize a match race between the Derby- and Belmont-winning stablemates Secretariat and Riva Ridge. The race was sponsored by the Philip Morris tobacco company and would be fittingly known as the Marlboro Cup. The inaugural running of the Marlboro Cup, which would also include Onion and several other horses, was held over a mile and one-eighth at Big Sandy. Secretariat did not disappoint, winning the race and setting a world record for the distance in the process.

Secretariat's final race at Belmont Park was the Man o' War Stakes, which was run over one and a half miles on the turf. Again, Big Red made the race his own, winning by five lengths over Tentam, setting a track record of 2:24:80. Secretariat retired at the end of his three-year-old season, earning Horse of the Year, champion three-year-old male and champion turf horse honors. According to NYRA data, Secretariat holds the fastest times to date in Belmont Park history at the half-mile, three-quarter-mile, one-mile, one-and-one-quarter-mile and one-and-one-half-mile fractions.

While Secretariat was taking the sports world by storm, another superstar arrived at the racecourse. Ruffian was a tall, two-year-old filly with the elegance of a dancer and the speed of a locomotive. Owned by Stuart Janney and trained by Frank Whiteley, Ruffian broke her maiden at Belmont in her first time out, demolishing the field by fifteen lengths and equaling the track record of 1:03 for five and a half furlongs. She then took the Fashion Stakes at Aqueduct by six and three-quarters lengths, once again equaling the existing track record. Ruffian capped off these wins with a nine-length victory in the Astoria Stakes and, for good measure, set a new stakes record in the Sorority Stakes at Monmouth in a time of 1:09.

The "Queen of the Fillies," as her fans dubbed her, had yet to be defeated, or even headed, in a single race. She continued her winning ways with a wire-to-wire romp at the six-furlong Spinaway Stakes at Saratoga, coming off a four-week layoff for a popped splint. Ruffian's winning time of

1:08:60 shattered the previous Spinaway record of 1:09:80 at the Spa set by Numbered Account in 1971. It also surpassed the time of 1:09:20 logged by Sopranist in 1945, when the Spinaway had been run at Belmont Park due to wartime restrictions. Hours after Ruffian's historic win, Secretariat's trainer Lucien Laurin allegedly told reporters, "As God as my judgment, this filly may be better than Secretariat!"[30]

Following her victory in the Spinaway, Ruffian was scheduled to run in the Frizette and Champagne Stakes, where she would face colts as well as fillies. However, Ruffian developed a fever prior to the Frizette and was forced to withdraw from the race. Soon after, it was discovered that the filly had sustained a hairline fracture in her right hind pastern, requiring eight weeks of stall rest. Ruffian would not race again until the following season.

The gallant filly's three-year-old debut occurred on Monday, April 14, 1974, at Belmont Park, where she handily won the eighth race on the card. According to the website Spilletta.com, "The other trainers with entries in the eighth race at Belmont probably would not have sent them to post, had they been given time to scratch, but Whiteley had done a masterful job of concealing his plans."[31]

Later in April, Ruffian headed to Aqueduct, where she won the Comely Stakes, setting a stakes record of 1:21:20 over seven furlongs. The filly was then entered in the NYRA Filly Triple Crown, which at that time consisted of the Acorn Stakes, the Mother Goose Stakes and the Coaching Club American Oaks. Again she virtually annihilated the competition, winning the Acorn by eight and a quarter lengths in a stakes-record time of 1:34:40 and following this victory with a stakes record of 1:47:80 in the Mother Goose. Ruffian cruised to victory by three lengths in the CCA Oaks, equaling the record time of 2:27:80.

Around this time, a match race was arranged between Ruffian and the reigning Kentucky Derby winner, Foolish Pleasure. According to sources, Ruffian had not been included in the original plan, which had been proposed as a rematch between the winners of each of that year's Triple Crown races. In response to this suggestion, the *Blood Horse* had written: "Until these colts are measured against Ruffian, none of them has much of a claim on the title of 3-year-old champion. Right now we do not believe that—even to escape a swarm of Brazil's hybrid African honeybees—any of these could catch up with the Stuart Janney's big filly [sic]."[32]

What had originated in thought as a three-horse race thus evolved into a duel between the sexes, with the nation's top filly taking on the leading American colt. A crowd of fifty thousand was in attendance on July 6, 1975, to watch the showdown over Big Sandy. With the filly leading at the half-mile mark, tragedy struck as Ruffian apparently took a misstep, fracturing both sesamoid bones in her right foreleg. Emergency surgery was performed to repair the injuries, but efforts to save the great filly were futile. While awakening from surgery, she began to thrash around, causing further irreparable damage to her legs and giving veterinarians no choice but to euthanize the superstar filly.

As a fitting tribute, Ruffian was buried near the flagpole at Belmont Park, with her nose pointing toward the finish line. In the days following her death, the NYRA flew its flag at half-staff in honor of the fallen champion. Additionally, a wreath constructed of 1,200 white carnations was placed on the filly's grave.

Ruffian's death shook the racing world to its core and reminded racegoers of the fragility of life. She is regarded as a legendary figure in the sport and holds her place alongside racing's all-time greats. The memories of her glorious era—and the beautiful, dark filly that could run like the wind—remain etched forever in the history of Belmont Park.

To this day, thousands of fans pay their respects to the immortal Secretariat and Ruffian, both of whom are forever memorialized on the grounds of Belmont Park. Flowers are often left to adorn Ruffian's grave site, which is surrounded by hedges that form a lush, emerald horseshoe. Secretariat's brilliance at Belmont Park is commemorated by a beautiful bronze statue, which stands in the paddock near the aged white pine tree. Each year, on Belmont Stakes day, the statue is draped with a blanket of white carnations—a lasting celebration of the greatest performance in the history of Belmont Park.

Chapter 13

A "SLEW" OF CHAMPIONS

The popularity of Secretariat and Ruffian drew legions of new fans to the sport. In the mid-1970s, horse racing enjoyed a resurgence in popularity, bolstered by the appeal of these equine celebrities. Fans flocked in droves to the new, modernized Belmont Park, and the horses did not disappoint.

A favorite of East Coast racing during this time was the great Forego, which had placed fourth behind Secretariat in the 1973 Kentucky Derby. Forego came into his own the following season, winning a series of key races that included the Woodward, the Brooklyn Handicap and the two-mile Jockey Club Gold Cup. As he was a gelding, Forego was not subject to early retirement and, while still campaigning at five years old, placed in all but one of his starts. After dominating in Aqueduct's Carter Handicap, Forego set a track record in the Brooklyn Handicap and capped it off with a win in the Suburban, carrying weights much greater than those of his competitors.

In 1976, Forego thrilled the crowd at Big Sandy when he won the Marlboro Cup while carrying a high weight of 137 pounds. He had contested the early lead with the younger Honest Pleasure, which carried twenty pounds less than Forego, before appearing to tire on the backstretch. In a thrilling display of speed and grit, Forego rallied from eighth place to defeat Honest Pleasure in a photo finish at the wire.

Forego's other wins as a six-year-old included the Brooklyn Handicap, Met Mile and Woodward Stakes races. The following season, he added yet two more accolades to his impressive resumé, winning another Met Mile and a fourth consecutive Woodward Stakes. In fifty-seven starts, Forego amassed thirty-four wins, nine seconds and seven thirds and retired with career earnings of $1,938,957.

As Forego was setting new records in 1977, a handsome seal brown colt arrived for the Belmont Stakes. His name was Seattle Slew, and he had first amazed racegoers during the prior season. As a juvenile, he had romped to a five-length win in his very first outing on Belmont's dirt track. Slew's other starts that season were equally impressive; these included an allowance race win followed by victory in the Champagne Stakes less than two weeks later, the latter by nearly ten lengths. Despite racing only three times that season, Seattle Slew would be deservedly named champion two-year-old colt.

As a three-year-old, Slew began his season with a proverbial bang, winning an allowance race at Hialeah and setting a track record for seven furlongs in the process. The colt proceeded to win the Flamingo Stakes and the Wood Memorial, two key Derby prep races, both by nearly four lengths. Despite displaying pre-race antics that would become his trademark, Slew ran well at Churchill Downs, solidifying his place in history with a one-and-three-quarter-length win over Run Dusty Run in the Derby. Two weeks later, at Pimlico, Slew held off multiple stakes winners Cormorant and Iron Constitution to capture the sought-after Preakness Stakes. It was then on to Big Sandy, where Slew and jockey Jean Cruguet dazzled the crowd to win the Belmont by a seemingly easy four lengths. Seattle Slew not only became the ninth Triple Crown winner in U.S. history but also the first to complete the series undefeated.

Following his Triple Crown win, Slew was defeated by the colt J.O. Tobin in the Swaps Stakes at Hollywood Park. This loss did little to tarnish the champion's reputation, and Slew was appropriately named Horse of the Year. In the off-season, however, the horse was sidelined with a serious illness that nearly claimed his life. The great champion defied the odds and returned to the racetrack in 1978.

By the time Seattle Slew arrived at Belmont Park for the Marlboro Cup in the summer of 1978, America had coronated a new Triple Crown champion, Affirmed. Following the Triple Crown drought that had plagued the 1950s and '60s, horse racing had been treated to consecutive Triple Crown wins.

The 1978 season was peppered with excitement from the start, owing to one of the greatest rivalries in the history of horse racing. Affirmed and his main rival, Alydar, were talented colts with very dissimilar styles of running. Affirmed, trained by Laz Barrera, won seven of his nine starts as a two-year-old under the guidance of teenage jockey Steve Cauthen. The colt was a front-runner that enjoyed having the lead, a style that appeared to serve him well. While Affirmed was most comfortable at the front of the pack, the Calumet-bred Alydar preferred to hang back before making his move. The differences in these two running styles made the meetings between Affirmed and Alydar especially exciting.

The two chestnut colts had first met at Belmont Park for the Youthful Stakes in 1977. The five-and-a-half-furlong outing had been Alydar's first start while Affirmed had already broken his maiden. Affirmed took the win in this first matchup between the two while the less experienced Alydar failed to challenge and placed fifth. This would be the only race that included both Affirmed and Alydar in which the two colts did not place first and second. The order of finish could vary; often Affirmed would prevail, and other times Alydar would be the winner, setting off a thrilling rivalry for the ages. By the end of their two-year-old season, the colts had met six times, with Affirmed taking four wins to Alydar's two and securing champion two-year-old colt honors.

Heading into the Triple Crown races, the two had taken separate paths. Alydar had a more stellar prep season and entered the Kentucky Derby as the six-to-five favorite. Under the historic twin spires at Churchill Downs, however, Affirmed held off his rival to capture the coveted garland of roses by one and one-half lengths. In the Preakness, Affirmed prevailed by a neck over Alydar in yet another breathtaking finish. When the two colts met in the Belmont Stakes, fans were mesmerized by an exciting stretch duel spanning the grueling mile and a half. Ultimately, Affirmed prevailed by a nose over Alydar to become America's eleventh Triple Crown winner. Alydar, for his part, was the first horse to place second in all three Triple Crown races, losing by a combined margin of less than two lengths. Interestingly, in the races in which he did not face Affirmed that season, Alydar maintained a perfect record.

In the months following his triumph in the Belmont Stakes, Affirmed would face Seattle Slew on two occasions at Belmont Park. In the Marlboro Cup, which was the first meeting between two Triple Crown winners on the track, Affirmed was sent off as the one-to-two betting favorite, with Slew the second choice at two-to-one. According to sources, Alydar was also originally scheduled to run in the race but had been withdrawn due to injury.

Slew, with jockey Angel Cordero Jr. on board, broke first, barreling out of the starting gate and leading through much of the race. Affirmed made a charge to catch the dark brown colt but was beaten by three lengths in a time of 1:45:80—less than a second short of the track record set by the immortal

Affirmed, 1978 Triple Crown champion. *Photo courtesy Adam Coglianese.*

Secretariat. A mere two weeks later, Slew defeated the colt Exceller, winner of several European races, by four lengths in the Woodward Stakes.

Seattle Slew and Affirmed would meet again that autumn in what is widely considered one of the most memorable runnings of the Jockey Club Gold Cup. The race was televised on national TV via the CBS network and was touted as a second duel between the Triple Crown champions. In the end, however, it was another colt that would prevail over Big Sandy to win the Jockey Club Gold Cup.

The speedy Seattle Slew set a blazing early pace, with Affirmed following closely in second. When Slew began to draw away, Affirmed's saddle slipped, and the colt became rank. Exceller, guided by the legendary Bill Shoemaker, suddenly made his move, galloping from twenty-two lengths back to enter into a stretch run with the tiring Triple Crown winner. Seattle Slew battled with every exhausting stride, ultimately losing to Exceller in a photo finish. The great Affirmed finished fifth.

While Slew and Affirmed lived out their lives as highly successful and treasured stallions, Exceller's story would end years later on a somber note.

After his racing and breeding careers had ended, the handsome white-faced bay died in a slaughterhouse in Sweden. His name now serves to bring awareness to the plight of retired Thoroughbreds through the Exceller Fund charity organization.

After three Triple Crowns in a mere six-year span, the crowning of a new champion was becoming something of a common occurrence. In 1979, the arrival of the colt Spectacular Bid gave credence to the expectation that another Triple Crown winner was on its way. The gray colt, known affectionately as the "Bid," had won the Champagne Stakes at Belmont during his juvenile season en route to capturing two-year-old colt honors. As a three-year-old, he returned to Belmont Park as the reigning Derby and Preakness champion, and fans believed him a worthy Triple Crown contender.

In the Belmont Stakes, however, the added distance proved too great a challenge, and the gallant colt ultimately finished third. Many attributed this loss to the fact that the horse had stepped on a safety pin in his stall; the pin had punctured the sole of the foot, causing pain and inflammation. Others blamed the defeat on a riding error by the young jockey Ronnie Franklin, who moved the colt quickly in the race. Regardless of the cause, the "Bid" was not destined for Triple Crown glory. The colt did, however, attain several other important victories during his stellar career. Under the guidance of a new rider, the legendary Bill Shoemaker, the Bid won the Marlboro Cup at Big Sandy in 1979. Later that season, he placed a game second behind Affirmed in the Jockey Club Gold Cup over one and a half miles. As a four-year-old, the Bid would be undefeated in a series of nine races, including the Woodward Stakes, which he won in a walkover.

The turn of the decade brought a bevy of new runners to Belmont Park, many of which were fan favorites. The year 1982 ushered in the victory of Conquistador Cielo, the first of five consecutive Belmont Stakes wins for trainer Woody Stephens. Widely respected within the industry, Stephens had garnered wins in both the Kentucky Derby and the Preakness, but the Belmont Stakes had eluded him thus far.

Conquistador Cielo, a bay colt, was sired by the distinguished Mr. Prospector, which carried the bloodlines of Nashua. After demonstrating talent as a juvenile in the Saratoga Special, Conquistador Cielo bypassed both the Derby and Preakness Stakes the following spring. Rather, trainer Stephens pointed the colt toward the Met Mile, where he would face several older horses on the Belmont dirt track. The colt rose to the lofty occasion, winning the race by seven lengths and setting a New York record of 1:33:00 in the process. The following Saturday, Conquistador Cielo won the Belmont Stakes over Derby champion Gato del Sol by a whopping fourteen lengths.

Just months after the victory of Conquistador Cielo, tragedy struck at Belmont Park in October's Jockey Club Gold Cup. While making his signature move in the stretch, the favored Timely Writer shattered his foreleg, devastating the hopes of racing fans at Belmont Park.

If talent had been correlated with longevity, Timely Writer would have lived to sire many champions. A son of Staff Writer out of the mare Timely Roman, the plain bay colt showed tremendous promise. Timely Writer had an "everyman" quality that reminded people of Seabiscuit. In addition to his talent, the horse was distinguished by the mere fact of his humble existence.

Timely Writer was owned by Peter and Francis Martin, two brothers who managed a meatpacking plant in Boston. The Martins maintained a string of horses under their Nitram Stable, a name derived from the backward spelling of "Martin." While their stable primarily consisted of claimers, the Martins dreamed of one day finding the proverbial "big horse." They found just that in Timely Writer, which was purchased for a mere $13,500 and began his career in a claiming race at Monmouth Park.

The Staff Writer colt raced at Saratoga in the summer of 1981 under the banner of trainer Dominic Imprescia. His first race at the Spa was the Saratoga Special, where he finished a game third. The winner of that race was the aforementioned Conquistador Cielo, which would go on to capture the 1982 Belmont Stakes. In contrast to Timely Writer, Conquistador Cielo had been sold for $150,000 as a yearling.

Timely Writer would return to Saratoga's track for the much-touted Hopeful Stakes. The favorite was the chestnut gelding Out of Hock, and little attention was paid to the Boston-based long shot. Ridden by jockey Roger Danjean, Timely Writer stalked the pace before roaring from the outside post in the stretch to overtake the favorite. Winning the Hopeful by a solid four lengths, Timely Writer established himself as a legitimate contender. This win, coupled with later victories in the Champagne Stakes at Belmont and the Florida Derby at Gulfstream Park, made Timely Writer a favorite for the Triple Crown races. In March 1982, the one-time claimer was the subject of a feature in *Sports Illustrated*.

The following month, rather than preparing for the Derby, Timely Writer was recovering from colic surgery at a veterinary hospital. Given odds of fifty-fifty merely to survive, he fought back valiantly and returned to training. At Saratoga that summer, he "toyed with a field of four older horses" and won the $32,000 Saratoga Hospital Purse by nearly three lengths. Bolstered by the cheers of adoring fans, Timely Writer finished the race in 1:21:60 despite little urging from jockey Jeffrey Fell.

After showing great promise in his later races, Timely Writer was pointed toward the Jockey Club Gold Cup at Belmont Park. It was to be his final race before retiring to stud duty, as the colt's breeding rights had been acquired by the famed Dr. William O. Reed. Sadly, it was not to be, as Timely Writer shattered his foreleg during the running of the Gold Cup and was euthanized on the track. Another horse, Johnny Dance, collided with the fallen champion and also sustained fatal injuries.

Timely Writer was buried near the American flag in the Belmont infield, in the area adjacent to the grave site of the immortal Ruffian. While fate prevented him from showing his full ability among the greats of the sport, Timely Writer is remembered fondly for the brilliance he showed in his brief lifetime.

Timely Writer's death was a poignant reminder that Thoroughbred racing is a sport of highs and lows. The sadness brought on by the loss of this valiant horse would remain at Belmont Park for years to come. In the meantime, there was great joy in New York, as fans celebrated trainer Woody Stephens's second consecutive Belmont Stakes win. The 1983 victory of Stephens's Caveat at Big Sandy was also emblematic, as the horse was owned by a partnership that included August Belmont IV.

Caveat did not demonstrate greatness from the start, and his juvenile season was less than stellar. The horse rebounded as a three-year-old, winning the Derby Trial at Churchill Downs and placing third in the Kentucky Derby. Piloted by Laffit Pincay Jr. (who had also ridden Conquistador Cielo), Caveat showed domination in the Belmont, winning the race by three and a half lengths over the favored Slew o' Gold. It would be the second consecutive Belmont trophy for the well-respected Woody Stephens.

Stephens's dominance of the Belmont would continue in the following year with the arrival of the colt Swale. The nearly black son of Seattle Slew had originally been overshadowed by his talented stablemate Devil's Bag, to which *Time* magazine had once referred as "the next Secretariat." Devil's Bag had set two records at Belmont Park as a juvenile and blazed to victories in both the Cowdin Stakes and the Champagne Stakes. For his part, Swale commanded notice with a win in the Futurity, which he capped off with a victory in the Saratoga Special.

While Devil's Bag was sidelined with an injury, Swale won the Kentucky Derby at Churchill Downs by three and a quarter lengths under jockey

Laffit Pincay. The colt was not at his best in the Preakness, and he finished a disappointing seventh. He rebounded strongly in the Belmont Stakes, however, dominating by four lengths to bring Stephens his third consecutive August Belmont trophy. This equaled the record set by trainer Frank McCabe, who won three consecutive Belmont Stakes races in the period from 1886 to 1888.

Eight days after his stunning Belmont Stakes win, Swale collapsed and died after being bathed on the Belmont Park backstretch. An autopsy failed to reveal any defects in the heart or aorta, and the cause of his death has remained shrouded in mystery. Swale's unexpected death, like those of Ruffian and Timely Writer, dealt a devastating blow to the racing industry and reminded fans and media of the fragility of these magnificent equine athletes.

While fans attempted to make sense out of Swale's untimely death, racing continued in all its highs and lows. In 1984, Woody Stephens continued his string of Belmont Stakes triumphs with the victory of Crème Fraiche. After bypassing the Kentucky Derby in May, Crème Fraiche became the first gelding to win the Belmont Stakes, which he accomplished in a thrilling victory over stablemate Stephan's Odyssey. Following this performance, Crème Fraiche went on to win consecutive runnings of the Jockey Club Gold Cup in 1986 and 1987, joining the immortal Nashua as the only Belmont Stakes champion to win two Jockey Club Gold Cup races.

Woody Stephens's success continued into the following year, when he won his fifth, and final, Belmont Stakes with Danzig Connection, which had previously won the Peter Pan Stakes with jockey Pat Day in the irons. Several days after Danzig Connection's victory, the NYRA presented Stephens with a wristwatch commemorating the trainer's five consecutive Belmont Stakes triumphs. According to sources, the watch was one of Stephens's prized possessions.

Woody Stephens, now a legend at Belmont Park, passed away in 1998 at the age of eighty-four. Several years earlier, Stephens had donated his five Belmont Stakes trophies, along with other artifacts, to the NYRA for a special display at Belmont Park. In recent years, a permanent exhibit called "Woody's Corner" was added to the first-floor clubhouse lobby. Situated under a grand arch, the display includes a large painting in which Stephens is depicted atop his stable pony; surrounding the pair, on canvas, are Stephens's five Belmont Stakes winners. Fans may visit the display to view the trophies, pay their respects and reminisce about the five-year period in which Woody Stephens made the Belmont Stakes his own.

Following the string of victories by Woody Stephens, Secretariat's son Risen Star won the 1988 Belmont Stakes by fourteen and three-quarters lengths over Kingpost in a blazing time of 2:26:40. Risen Star thus joined a growing list of Belmont Stakes champions that had, in fact, been sired by another Belmont winner.

Belmont Stakes Champions That Sired Winners of the Belmont	
Sire/Belmont Win	**Offspring/Belmont Win**
Duke of Magenta (1878)	Eric (1889)
Spendthrift (1879)	Hastings (1896)
Hastings (1896)	Masterman (1902)
Commando (1901)	Peter Pan (1907)
	Colin (1908)
The Finn (1915)	Zev (1923)
Man o' War (1920)	American Flag (1925)
	Crusader (1926)
	War Admiral (1937)
Gallant Fox (1930)	Omaha (1935)
	Granville (1936)
Count Fleet (1943)	Counterpoint (1951)
	One Count (1952)
Sword Dancer (1959)	Damascus (1967)
Secretariat (1973)	Risen Star (1988)
Seattle Slew (1977)	Swale (1984)
	A.P. Indy (1992)

In the same season in which Risen Star won the Belmont Stakes, a two-year-old colt by the name of Easy Goer commanded attention at the racetrack. The colt had made his debut at Big Sandy in a maiden juvenile sprint but, despite a game effort, was beaten by a nose at the wire. Easy Goer avenged that defeat at Belmont later in the season, when he won the Champagne Stakes by an imposing four lengths over the colt Is It True. Easy Goer's time of 1:34:80 for the mile was the fourth fastest in Champagne Stakes history, following the records set by Vitriolic, Seattle Slew and Devil's Bag. Easy Goer had also won an allowance race at Belmont Park over six and a half furlongs; when the colt ran the running one-fifth of a second off the track record in 1:15:40, trainer "Shug" McGaughey noted that he "knew [he] was training something special."

The 1989 Belmont Stakes could have served as a coronation for the black colt Sunday Silence, which narrowly defeated Easy Goer in both the

Kentucky Derby and the Preakness. Prior to the Derby, the media had set up an "East versus West" rivalry, similar to those in the past touting "Nashua versus Swaps" and "War Admiral versus Seabiscuit." The eastern-bred Easy Goer, with a string of blazing fast victories, was perceived to be the superior horse and was thus selected as the betting line favorite. Galloping on a muddy track at Churchill Downs, however, Easy Goer appeared to be lacking his usual speed, and Sunday Silence handily beat him by two and a half lengths.

The Preakness Stakes was highly anticipated as a rematch between the two colts, with Easy Goer expected to recover his usual luster. The media proclaimed the event "the race of the half century," and fans were delighted when the two colts dueled in a thrilling stretch run at Pimlico. In the end, the westerner Sunday Silence prevailed by a nose, heading to Belmont Park with a chance to become the next Triple Crown champion.

With the Derby and Preakness to his name, Sunday Silence was now deemed the odds-on favorite on Belmont Stakes day. The top performance, however, was made by Easy Goer, which dominated his rival by an impressive eight lengths. His winning time of 2:26.00 was the second fastest to date, lagging behind only the immortal Secretariat.

Easy Goer, winner of the 1989 Belmont Stakes and Jockey Club Gold Cup. *Photo courtesy Bud Morton.*

Easy Goer's later performances would place him in elite company. In addition to winning the Travers and Whitney at Saratoga and setting a new track record in the Gotham Stakes at Aqueduct, the colt defeated older horses in both the Woodward and the Jockey Club Gold Cup at Belmont Park. In doing so, Easy Goer became the sole champion in history to win the combination of the Travers, Whitney, Woodward and Jockey Club Gold Cup races. He also joined Kelso and Slew o' Gold as the only horses to have won the Whitney, Woodward and Jockey Club Gold Cup races in the same year, becoming the only one to do so as a three-year-old. As the *New York Times* proclaimed after the colt's Jockey Club Gold Cup win, "It did not take long for Easy Goer to prove he is made of strong stuff."[33]

Chapter 14

FAN FAVORITES

The year 1990 brought a new dynamic to Belmont Park with the arrival of its first-ever Breeders' Cup Championships. Established in 1982 by John R. Gaines, the Breeders' Cup was developed as an annual weekend of championship racing for Thoroughbreds from all over the world. Offering a series of different races during one weekend, horses could compete by age and sex in various categories over dirt and turf. The Breeders' Cup would be held at a different racetrack each year, with its inaugural running held in 1984 at Hollywood Park. Its first occurrence at Belmont Park took place on October 27, 1990.

The 1990 Classic, the top race on the Breeders' Cup card, was won by Frances Genter's bay colt Unbridled in a time of 2:02:20 under jockey Pat Day. Sadly, the joy of this event was marred by the fatal breakdown of the much-loved filly Go For Wand in the Ladies' Classic earlier that day. The gravely injured Go For Wand was euthanized on the Belmont track and was buried at Saratoga, the site of two of her greatest victories. As a tribute to the champion filly, the Maskette Stakes at Belmont Park was renamed the Go For Wand Handicap; it would be moved to Saratoga in 1994.

In 1995, the Breeders' Cup Championships returned to Belmont for a second time. The highlight of the event that year was the classic victory of the great Cigar in a stakes record time of 1:59:58. Cigar had raced successfully at Belmont Park earlier that season, when he won both the Woodward Stakes and the Jockey Club Gold Cup. The Breeders' Cup Classic victory marked the ending of a perfect season, during which the colt had won all

Left: The champion filly Go For Wand. *Photo courtesy Bud Morton.*

Below: Skip Away, two-time winner of the Jockey Club Gold Cup. *Photo courtesy Allison Pareis.*

of his ten starts. Cigar's winning streak continued into the following season, in which he captured, among other races, a second consecutive Woodward Stakes. This race was to be Cigar's final victory that season, as he would lose by a head to the great Skip Away in the Jockey Club Gold Cup in a thrilling stretch drive. Cigar would retire at the end of his six-year-old season as America's leading money winner.

Cigar's foil in the Gold Cup, the handsome gray Skip Away, would win several other races at Belmont Park in 1996 and 1997. He had narrowly lost the 1996 Belmont Stakes to a game Editor's Note as a three-year-old but had rebounded to win the Haskell at Monmouth Park before defeating Cigar in the Gold Cup. After a rough start at the early part of the 1997 season, Skip Away was paired with a new jockey, Jerry Bailey, who would guide the colt to nine consecutive victories. Among the stallion's wins in 1997 was a second consecutive Jockey Club Gold Cup at Belmont Park.

Prior to Skip Away's victory in the 1997 Gold Cup, another gray colt had garnered attention when he arrived at Belmont Park. Trained by Bob Baffert and ridden by Gary Stevens, Silver Charm was highly favored to become the first Triple Crown winner in nineteen years. It was not to be, however, as the stunning colt was passed by Touch Gold and jockey Chris McCarron on the far outside. Touch Gold won the Belmont Stakes by three-quarters of a length, dashing the public's hopes of ending the Triple Crown drought. This scenario would virtually repeat itself the following season, when Derby and Preakness champion Real Quiet was defeated by Victory Gallop in the Belmont Stakes.

Real Quiet, nicknamed the "Fish" by trainer Bob Baffert, had won both the Derby and Preakness in commanding fashion with jockey Kent Desormeaux aboard. The media was quick to anoint the colt as the new successor to Affirmed, owing to his convincing performance in the Preakness Stakes at Pimlico. Once again, however, Big Sandy proved a source of disappointment, as Real Quiet was passed narrowly at the finish line by Victory Gallop. Many blamed the narrow defeat on jockey error, as some felt that Desormeaux had simply moved the colt out too quickly. As it had done so many times before, the Belmont Stakes had cost another horse a chance at racing immortality.

The decade would close at Belmont Park with a third consecutive Triple Crown near miss. In 1999, the chestnut colt Charismatic arrived at Big Sandy as the reigning Derby-Preakness champion. The horse had a rather interesting back story, as he had been passed over by several jockeys—including Jerry Bailey, Laffit Pincay, Chris McCarron and Mike Smith—before Chris Antley finally agreed to ride him. Antley was attempting a comeback to the sport, having taken a hiatus from riding while battling substance abuse problems.

Trained by the famed D. Wayne Lukas, Charismatic was sent off on Derby day as a thirty-one-to-one longshot. He surprised the bettors and pundits alike, besting the favored Menifee by a head to win the garland of roses. He repeated this victory at Pimlico, where he once again finished ahead of Menifee, this time by one and a half lengths.

Heading into the Belmont Stakes, Charismatic was sent off as the two-to-one favorite over Menifee, with the rivalry between the two colts sparking comparisons to Affirmed and Alydar. As the race wound down, it appeared as if America might at last have another Triple Crown winner as Charismatic grabbed the lead in the final furlong. Suddenly and without apparent reason, the horse faded to third behind Lemon Drop Kid and Vision and Verse. Immediately after crossing the finish line, jockey Antley dismounted and grabbed Charismatic's wobbly left front leg. The reason for the defeat was now sadly apparent.

Antley later told reporters that he had sensed that something was wrong during the final furlong and had thus eased the horse to avoid a breakdown. X-rays determined that the horse's leg was indeed fractured, and thanks to Antley's heroic efforts, the horse survived and became a breeding stallion.

The quest for the Triple Crown would continue into the new millennium.

Chapter 15

THE NEW MILLENNIUM

The arrival of the year 2000 brought new hope to the racing industry. No horse had won the Triple Crown since Affirmed in 1978, well before the births of racing's younger fans. There were many theories as to why this Triple Crown drought had occurred. Many felt that horses were no longer being bred for stamina and that they were too fragile to soundly conquer the imposing Big Sandy track. Some fans blamed the drought on various trainers, who purposely entered fresh horses in the Belmont Stakes in an attempt to spoil a possible Triple Crown. Others suggested that the weeks between the Triple Crown races should be extended, even though doing so might jeopardize the purity of the feat. The message was clear: America was clamoring for a Triple Crown champion.

While Americans hoped and prayed for a successor to Affirmed, the Breeders' Cup returned in 2001 for a third session at Belmont Park. The event was a coronation of the colt Tiznow, which captured his second consecutive running of the Breeders' Cup Classic. Tiznow, which was known for his prowess on dirt, had won the 2000 edition of the Classic at Churchill Downs under famed jockey Chris McCarron. At Belmont Park, the four-year-old bested the bay colt Sakhee, winner of the Prix de l'Arc de Triomphe in France. To date, Tiznow remains the only two-time winner of the Breeders' Cup Classic.

In the year following Tiznow's historic victory, the colt War Emblem arrived at the Belmont Stakes in a valiant attempt to quash the Triple Crown drought. After winning the Derby and Preakness combination, War Emblem and jockey Victor Espinoza seemed destined for glory in the Belmont Stakes. A record crowd of 103,222 flocked to Belmont Park, hoping to witness history in the making. As the starting gate opened in the Belmont Stakes, however, War Emblem stumbled and fell behind the leaders. The colt was unable to gain command of the race, which was ultimately won by the dark bay colt, Sarava, and jockey Edgar Prado. At odds of seventy-to-one, Sarava became the longest shot in history to win the Belmont Stakes.

In 2003, an unlikely hero called Funny Cide made his own attempt at Triple Crown glory. Funny Cide, a chestnut horse owned by a group of high school buddies, made headlines when he won the Kentucky Derby over the favored Empire Maker by one and a half lengths. With this victory, he became the first gelding since 1929 to win the Kentucky Derby and the first New York–bred horse to capture the race. Funny Cide followed this win with a victory in the Preakness, setting off a deluge of Triple Crown mania.

A rainstorm on the day before the Belmont Stakes rendered Big Sandy deep and soggy. Jockey Santos kept Funny Cide close to the rail, which, after heavy rain, was the deepest part of the track, and had trouble rating the horse as he pulled on the reins. With his chestnut coat masked by splatters of mud, the gelding finished a disappointing third behind the energetic Empire Maker and Ten Most Wanted, neither of which had competed in the Preakness Stakes. The disappointed crowd booed Empire Maker as he was led into the Belmont Stakes winner's circle. In response, Empire Maker's trainer, Bobby Frankel, explained, "Thirty years [since Secretariat] and twenty-five [since Affirmed won the Triple Crown]. Sometimes you think these things are destiny, and you don't want to have destiny against you."[34]

The following year, the then-undefeated colt Smarty Jones brought "Triple Crown mania" to new heights when he won the Derby and Preakness Stakes under the guidance of jockey Stewart Elliott. As fans hoped that this horse would be the one to finally end the Triple Crown drought, Smarty Jones became a national celebrity, appearing on the covers of magazines such as *Sports Illustrated*.

The proverbial racing gods were unkind to Smarty Jones over Big Sandy, just as they had been to so many others before him. Emerging from the starting gate, Smarty set a blistering early pace that he was unable to maintain for the one and a half miles. He was caught by the more distance-favoring Birdstone, which, at odds of thirty-six to one, rallied from behind to win the Belmont Stakes trophy. The now-defeated Smarty Jones would never race again, owing to chronic foot soreness.

Birdstone was owned by Marylou Whitney (widow of Cornelius Vanderbilt Whitney), a much-admired figure in New York racing. The colt would go on to win the Travers Stakes at Saratoga that summer and would later sire, among others, 2009 Belmont Stakes and Jockey Club Gold Cup champion Summer Bird.

The Breeders' Cup returned to Belmont Park in 2005, highlighted by the victory of Saint Liam in the Classic. The five-year-old colt had also won the 2005 Woodward Stakes. The Classic would mark Saint Liam's farewell to racing, having achieved nine wins, six places and one show in twenty starts and earning more than $4.5 million. Sadly, Saint Liam would be fatally injured in a stable accident while standing at stud the following year. He did sire a number of offspring before his death, including, most notably, the 2011 Horse of the Year, Havre de Grace.

In 2006, the colt Bernardini won the Jockey Club Gold Cup as part of a winning season that also included the Preakness and Travers Stakes. While Bernardini had impressively won the Preakness by five and a quarter lengths, his triumph was overshadowed by the tragic breakdown of beloved Kentucky Derby champion Barbaro. Following the Preakness, Bernardini's owner Sheik Mohammed kept the colt out of the Belmont Stakes, marking only the fourth time in sixty years in which both the Derby and Preakness winners were absent from the race.

After winning both the Jim Dandy and Travers Stakes in impressive fashion at Saratoga, the son of 1992 Belmont Stakes winner, A.P. Indy, prevailed over three older horses in the Jockey Club Gold Cup, earning a Beyer speed figure of 117 for his efforts. Bernardini would be named champion three-year-old colt at the end of the season and has become one of the premier young stallions of the modern age.

Another of A.P. Indy's offspring, the filly Rags to Riches, made history in the 2007 Belmont Stakes when she became the first filly to win the race since Tanya in 1905. A flashy white-faced chestnut, Rags to Riches made her first start against males in the Belmont, ultimately defeating Preakness winner Curlin by a head at the wire. The two had battled head to head at the top of the stretch, with the game filly besting Curlin in one of the most memorable duels in history. On television, announcer Tom Durkin narrated the play-by-play:

> *Here comes Hard Spun. And Curlin is coming through in between horses! And Rags to Riches is coming with a four-wide sweep! And Tiago is in behind them. And at the top of the stretch, a filly is in front at the Belmont! But Curlin is right there with her! These two, in a battle of the sexes at the Belmont Stakes! It is Curlin on the inside—Rags to Riches on the outside.*

A desperate finish: Rags to Riches and Curlin! They're coming down to the wire. It's gonna be very close! And it's gonna be…a filly in the Belmont!

Following his loss to Rags to Riches, Stonestreet Stables's Curlin won a number of key races and would retire in 2008 as North America's first $10 million career earner. His victories included consecutive runnings of the Jockey Club Gold Cup at Belmont Park in 2007 and 2008. In one of the most brilliant runnings of the Gold Cup, Curlin defeated the colt Lawyer Ron by a neck in 2007 after a stretch duel over Big Sandy. Completing the race in 2:01:20, Curlin earned a Beyer speed figure of 114 for his effort. The following September, Curlin defeated Wanderin Boy by three-quarters of a length over a sloppy track to win his second Gold Cup and overtake Cigar's standing as North America's all-time money winner.

Shortly before Curlin won his second Gold Cup, the colt Big Brown arrived at Belmont Park with a mission. Fresh off victories in the Derby and Preakness, Big Brown would attempt to achieve what War Emblem, Funny Cide and Smarty Jones had failed to do—become the first Triple Crown winner since Affirmed in 1978.

Named in honor of the brown uniforms worn by the United Parcel Service, Big Brown had begun his three-year-old season after having not raced in a period of six months. This raised questions for many who followed a more traditional schedule and doubted that the colt would be fit to race. The horse proved his critics wrong, winning the Florida Derby by five lengths under jockey Kent Desormeaux. In the Kentucky Derby on May 3, 2008, Big Brown became the first horse since 1929 to win the race from the twentieth starting gate. The victory was tempered by tragedy, however, as second-place finisher Eight Belles sustained fatal injuries and had to be euthanized on the track at Churchill Downs.

Big Brown continued his winning ways in the Preakness, which was only the fifth career start for the colt. He won the race by five and a quarter lengths over Macho Again, becoming the fourth undefeated winner of the Derby-Preakness combination. Following this win, it was discovered that the horse had developed a quarter crack in his left front hoof. In preparation for the Belmont, the hoof was sutured with steel wire, and a patch was applied to the hoof by the horse's farrier. Big Brown's trainer, Rick Dutrow, appeared confident that the horse's soundness would be unaffected by this injury.

Despite the patched hoof, Big Brown was sent off as the betting favorite at odds of three to ten. The colt was rank in the first part of the race, however, and jockey Desormeaux appeared to encounter difficulty in rating him. Desormeaux, feeling that something was wrong with the horse, pulled him up; this marked the first time in the history of the Belmont Stakes in which a Triple Crown contender failed to complete the race. The Belmont Stakes was ultimately won by Da' Tara, which galloped away with a five-and-a-quarter-length victory. It was later revealed that Big Brown's shoe had been displaced during the race, causing the horse discomfort and likely accounting for his unusual behavior. Big Brown would go on to win his next two starts, the Haskell Invitational and the Monmouth Stakes, before retiring to stallion duty.

In 2009, Stonestreet Stables's Rachel Alexandra drew a following at Belmont Park when she arrived to compete in the Mother Goose Stakes. A dark bay three-year-old filly with distinctive white facial markings, Rachel had made history at Churchill Downs with an unprecedented victory by twenty and one-quarter lengths in the historic Kentucky Oaks. She followed that win with a triumph in the Preakness Stakes, where she thwarted a late charge by the reigning Derby winner, Mine That Bird. With this victory, Rachel Alexandra became the first filly to win the Preakness since Nellie Morse in 1924.

Following her Preakness win, Rachel was shipped to Belmont Park, where she won the Mother Goose Stakes by nineteen and a quarter lengths, shattering the existing stakes record in a time of 1:46:33. This win also surpassed the margin of victory of thirteen and a half lengths that had been set by the immortal Ruffian in 1975, prompting comparisons between the two fillies.

On the heels of her victory at Belmont, Rachel headed to Monmouth Park, where she became the second filly in history to win the Haskell Invitational. Rachel achieved a Beyer speed rating of 116 for this victory, the highest of any horse in North America that season. On September 5, the "super filly" continued her domination as she held off a late charge by Macho Again to become the first female ever to win the Woodward Stakes, which had been moved to Saratoga. This win made Rachel the first three-year-old filly since 1887 to win a grade-one dirt race against older males. It was the ninth consecutive win for Rachel Alexandra, which capped off the season by being named Horse of the Year.

In the years from 2009 through 2011, the Triple Crown season was characterized by a trend in which no single horse won more than one of the three races. In 2009, following the victories of Mine That Bird in the Derby and Rachel Alexandra in the Preakness, the chestnut colt Summer Bird was victorious in the Belmont Stakes. The chestnut son of Birdstone prevailed in the Travers Stakes at Saratoga that summer and placed second behind Rachel Alexandra in the Haskell Invitational before heading back to Belmont for the Jockey Club Gold Cup.

While he would not face Rachel in the Gold Cup, Summer Bird fought off a worthy challenger in the talented Quality Road, which had set track records while winning the Florida Derby and Amsterdam Stakes. The two colts dueled in a long-stretch run over Big Sandy, with Summer Bird ultimately besting Quality Road by a length. In doing so, Summer Bird became the first three-year-old since Easy Goer to win the combination of the Belmont Stakes, the Travers and the Jockey Club Gold Cup.

The 2010 Belmont Stakes was won by the chestnut colt Drosselmeyer, a son of the stallion Distorted Humor, which had also sired Funny Cide. That season, Derby winner Super Saver and Preakness champion Lookin at Lucky were both absent from the Belmont, leaving the field virtually wide open. Sent off at betting odds of thirteen-to-one, Drosselmeyer defeated a field of eleven other starters, carrying veteran jockey Mike Smith to his first-ever Belmont Stakes victory. In another first, the win brought trainer Bill Mott his only triumph to date in a Triple Crown series race. More than a year after this victory, on November 5, 2011, Drosselmeyer won the million Breeders' Cup Classic at Churchill Downs.

Prior to Drosselmeyer's Breeders' Cup win, trainer Kelly Breen's Ruler on Ice became the second gelding in history, behind Crème Fraiche, to capture the Belmont Stakes trophy. The chestnut gelding had entered the race as a twenty-four-to-one longshot, having raced in neither the Derby nor the Preakness. Ruler on Ice completed the Belmont in 2:30:88, defeating both the Derby winner, Animal Kingdom, and Preakness champion, Shackleford, over a sloppy track. The gelding would return to Belmont Park the following year for the Jockey Club Gold Cup, where he challenged the front runners before being pulled up due to a slight lameness. Following his Belmont Stakes victory, Ruler on Ice would win only one other start—a claiming race at Aqueduct in January 2013.

In 2012, "Triple Crown mania" returned to full force with the Derby and Preakness victories of another chestnut colt, I'll Have Another, which was owned by businessman J. Paul Reddam and trained by Doug O'Neill. After a rather undistinguished two-year-old season, which included a sixth-place finish in Saratoga's Hopeful Stakes, the colt rebounded to win two key Derby prep races at Santa Anita in California. These included a game defeat of the favorite, Creative Cause, by a nose in the Santa Anita Derby, which bolstered him into the spotlight as a Kentucky Derby contender.

I'll Have Another works on the Belmont track. *Photo courtesy Jessie Holmes.*

Sent off at Churchill Downs at odds of fifteen to one, I'll Have Another bested the Bob Baffert-trained Bodemeister by a length and a half to win the prestigious Run for the Roses. In doing so, he became the first horse in history to win the Derby from post position nineteen. He capped off this victory with a win in the Preakness, defeating a game Bodemeister by a neck at the wire.

The victories of I'll Have Another sent the media into a frenzy. The colt became a favorite among fans, who enjoyed his seemingly heartwarming backstory. His jockey, Mario Gutierrez, was a virtual newcomer to the sport, and the Derby marked his first-ever Triple Crown start as a rider. Additionally, I'll Have Another was led to the post by the retired champion Lava Man, which now served as the colt's stable pony. Fans compared the horse's chestnut coloring to that of Secretariat and Affirmed and saw that as a sign that the horse would become the next Triple Crown winner.

I'll Have Another was entered in the Belmont Stakes and was observed working out over the dirt track in the days leading up to the race. When the post positions were drawn, the colt drew the eleventh position, emerging from the outside of the field of twelve runners. The media followed the horse's every move, with newspapers coronating him as the successor to the great Affirmed.

One day prior to the Belmont Stakes, trainer Doug O'Neill shocked the masses when he announced that I'll Have Another would not run in the race. A press conference was scheduled, during which O'Neill reported that the horse had been plagued with soreness in a front tendon. Rather than risking further injury, the horse would be immediately retired from racing. As such, I'll Have Another joined the ranks of Burgoo King in 1932 and Bold Venture in 1936, both of which had been scratched from the Belmont Stakes after having won the Kentucky Derby and Preakness.

Prior to the running of the race, a retirement ceremony was held for I'll Have Another in the Belmont winner's circle, during which the public was allowed to pay their respects to the champion and his connections. In the absence of I'll Have Another and Bodemeister (which was pointed toward summer racing at Saratoga), the Belmont Stakes became a thrilling contest between Phyllis Wyeth's Union Rags and the Bob Baffert–trained colt, Paynter. Union Rags was trained by Michael Matz, the former Olympic show jumping champion who had guided Barbaro to victory in the 2006 Kentucky Derby. The handsome Union Rags was a sentimental favorite among fans who had followed Matz since his show jumping days and subsequent connection with the ill-fated Barbaro. Union Rags had met with success at Belmont Park during the prior season, when he won the Champagne Stakes by five lengths over a front-running Alpha. A favorite to be named champion two-year-old colt, Union Rags had lost the title to the near-white colt Hansen, which had bested him by a head in the Breeders' Cup Juvenile.

Union Rags had a disappointing trip in the Kentucky Derby, during which he rallied from the back of the pack to finish seventh. Both trainer and owner opted to keep the colt out of the Preakness and instead pointed him toward the longer-distance Belmont Stakes. With a new jockey, the veteran John Velasquez, Union Rags was sent off as the co-favorite with the Irish-bred Dullahan and broke well as guided by the experienced hands of Velasquez. Allowing the speedy Paynter to set the pace, Velasquez steadily moved Union Rags along on the inside rail, ultimately overtaking the Baffert colt by a neck in the final strides. A new Belmont Stakes champion had been crowned.

While there would be no Triple Crown champion in 2012, fans delighted in the display of heart shown by Union Rags and Paynter, as well as that of the dashing colt Flat Out, which won his second consecutive Jockey Club Gold Cup that October.

MULTIPLE WINNERS OF THE JOCKEY CLUB GOLD CUP	
Horse	**Years Won**
Mad Hatter	1921, 1922
Dark Secret	1933, 1934
Firethorn	1935, 1937
Nashua	1955, 1956
Kelso	1960, 1961, 1962, 1963, 1964
Shuvee	1970, 1971
Slew o' Gold	1983, 1984
Crème Fraiche	1986, 1987
Skip Away	1996, 1997
Curlin	2007, 2008
Flat Out	2011, 2012

Decades have passed since a new Triple Crown champion emerged at Belmont Park, but the excitement generated at the racetrack continues to know no bounds. More than one hundred years after the founding of the track, the dream of August Belmont continues to pervade its vast surroundings. Fans flock in droves to the great racecourse, where horses remain challenged by the vast dimensions of the track. Belmont Park remains, as the *New York Times* formerly noted, "the most magnificently appointed racing plant on the American continent."

Appendix A

TRACK RECORDS

	MAIN TRACK			
Distance	**Horse**	**Weight**	**Time**	**Date**
5F	Kelly Kip	114	0:55:75	6/21/1996
5½F	Mike's Classic	119	1:02:26	6/20/2004
6F	Artax	120	1:07:66	10/16/1999
6½F	Super Shape (ARG)	120	1:14:46	10/21/2009
6½F	Bear Fan	121	1:14:46	6/5/2004
7F	Left Bank	121	1:20:17	7/4/2002
7½F	Commentator	119	1:27:44	9/24/2004
1M	Najran	113	1:32:24	5/7/2003
1¹⁄₁₆M	Birdrun	117	1:39:38	10/21/2009
1⅛M	Secretariat	124	1:45:40	9/15/1973
1³⁄₁₆M	Lueders	111	1:56:00	6/24/1982
1¼M	In Excess (IRE)	119	1:58:33	7/4/1991
1⅜M	Victoriously	118	2:14:72	10/16/1997
1½M	Secretariat	126	2:24:00	6/9/1973
1⅝M	Man o' War	126	2:40:80	9/4/1920

WIDENER TURF COURSE				
Distance	**Horse**	**Weight**	**Time**	**Date**
6F	Keep The Faith (AUS)	120	1:06:82	7/24/2005
7F	Officialpermission	112	1:19:88	7/23/2000
1M	Elusive Quality	117	1:31:63	7/4/1998
1⅟₁₆M	Fortitude	112	1:38:53	9/6/1997
1¼M	Honey Dear	112	2:03:80	10/10/1962
1⅜M	Influent	120	2:11:06	7/13/1997
1½M	Fantastic Light	126	2:24:36	10/27/2001
2M	King's General (GB)	112	3:20:40	7/4/1983

INNER TURF COURSE				
Distance	**Horse**	**Weight**	**Time**	**Date**
6F	Gantry	121	1:06:87	6/23/2011
1⅟₁₆M	Roman Envoy	117	1:39:38	5/23/1992
1⅛M	Shakespeare	114	1:45:06	9/11/2005
1¼M	Paradise Creek	124	1:57:79	6/11/1994
1⅜M	With Approval	118	2:10:26	6/17/1990

Source: NYRA

TRIPLE CROWN NEAR MISSES

Year	Horse	Belmont Finish
1932	Burgoo King	Did not start
1936	Bold Venture	Did not start
1944	Pensive	2nd
1958	Tim Tam	2nd
1961	Carry Back	7th
1964	Northern Dancer	3rd
1966	Kauai King	4th
1968	**Forward Pass	2nd
1969	Majestic Prince	2nd
1971	Canonero II	4th
1979	Spectacular Bid	3rd

Year	Horse	Belmont Finish
1981	Pleasant Colony	3rd
1987	Alysheba	4th
1989	Sunday Silence	2nd
1997	Silver Charm	2nd
1998	Real Quiet	2nd
1999	Charismatic	3rd
2002	War Emblem	8th
2003	Funny Cide	3rd
2004	Smarty Jones	2nd
2008	Big Brown	Did not finish
2012	I'll Have Another	Did not start

**Won on disqualification.

Source: horse-races.net

WINNERS OF THE BELMONT STAKES SINCE 1867

Year	Winner	Jockey	Trainer	Owner	Time
2012	Union Rags	John Velazquez	Michael Matz	Phyllis M. Wyeth	2:30:42
2011	Ruler on Ice	Jose Valdivia Jr.	Kelly Breen	George and Lori Hall	2:30:88
2010	Drosselmeyer	Mike Smith	William Mott	WinStar Farm LLC	2:31:57
2009	Summer Bird	Kent Desormeaux	Tim Ice	Kalarikkal & Vilasini Jayaraman	2:27:54
2008	Da'Tara	Alan Garcia	Nick Zito	Robert V. LaPenta	2:29:65
2007	Rags to Riches ‡	John Velazquez	Todd Pletcher	M. Tabor & D. Smith	2:28:74
2006	Jazil	Fernando Jara	Kiaran McLaughlin	Shadwell Farm	2:27:81
2005	Afleet Alex	Jeremy Rose	Timothy Ritchey	Cash is King LLC	2:28:75
2004	Birdstone	Edgar Prado	Nick Zito	Marylou Whitney Stables	2:27:50
2003	Empire Maker	Jerry Bailey	Robert Frankel	Juddmonte Farms	2:28:26
2002	Sarava	Edgar Prado	Kenneth McPeek	New Phoenix Stable	2:29:71
2001	Point Given	Gary Stevens	Bob Baffert	The Thoroughbred Corp.	2:26:80
2000	Commendable	Pat Day	D. Wayne Lukas	Bob & Beverly Lewis	2:31:20
1999	Lemon Drop Kid	Jose Santos	Scotty Schulhofer	Jeanne G. Vance	2:27:80
1998	Victory Gallop	Gary Stevens	W. Elliott Walden	Prestonwood Farm	2:29:00
1997	Touch Gold	Chris McCarron	David Hofmans	Frank Stronach	2:28:80
1996	Editor's Note	Rene R. Douglas	D. Wayne Lukas	Overbrook Farm	2:28:80
1995	Thunder Gulch	Gary Stevens	D. Wayne Lukas†	Michael Tabor	2:32:00
1994	Tabasco Cat	Pat Day	D. Wayne Lukas	Reynolds/Overbrook	2:26:80
1993	Colonial Affair	Julie Krone	Scotty Schulhofer	Centennial Farms	2:29:80
1992	A.P. Indy	Ed Delahoussaye	Neil Drysdale	Tomonori Tsurumaki	2:26:13
1991	Hansel	Jerry Bailey	Frank L. Brothers	Lazy Lane Farm	2:28:00
1990	Go And Go	Michael Kinane	Dermot K. Weld	Moyglare Stud Farm	2:27:20
1989	Easy Goer	Pat Day	C.R. McGaughey III	Ogden Phipps	2:26:00
1988	Risen Star	Ed Delahoussaye	Louie J. Roussel III	Louie J. Roussel III	2:26:40
1987	Bet Twice	Craig Perret	Jimmy Croll	Blanche P. Levy	2:28:20
1986	Danzig Connection	Chris McCarron	Woody Stephens	Henryk de Kwiatkowski	2:29:80
1985	Creme Fraiche	Eddie Maple	Woody Stephens	Brushwood Stables	2:27:00
1984	Swale	Laffit Pincay Jr.	Woody Stephens	Claiborne Farm	2:27:20

Year	Winner	Jockey	Trainer	Owner	Time
1983	Caveat	Laffit Pincay, Jr.	Woody Stephens	August Belmont IV	2:27:80
1982	Conquistador Cielo	Laffit Pincay, Jr.	Woody Stephens	Henryk de Kwiatkowski	2:28:20
1981	Summing	George Martens	Luis Barrera	Charles T. Wilson, Jr.	2:29:00
1980	Temperence Hill	Eddie Maple	Joseph B. Cantey	Loblolly Stable	2:29:80
1979	Coastal	Ruben Hernandez	David A. Whiteley	William Haggin Perry	2:28:60
1978	Affirmed †	Steve Cauthen	Laz Barrera	Harbor View Farm	2:26:80
1977	Seattle Slew †	Jean Cruguet	William H. Turner, Jr.	Karen L. Taylor	2:29:60
1976	Bold Forbes	Angel Cordero, Jr.	Laz Barrera	E. Rodriguez Tizol	2:29:00
1975	Avatar	Bill Shoemaker	Tommy Doyle	Arthur A. Seeligson, Jr.	2:28:20
1974	Little Current	Miguel A. Rivera	Lou Rondinello	Darby Dan Farm	2:29:20
1973	Secretariat †	Ron Turcotte	Lucien Laurin	Meadow Stable	2:24:00
1972	Riva Ridge	Ron Turcotte	Lucien Laurin	Meadow Stud	2:28:00
1971	Pass Catcher	Walter Blum	Eddie Yowell	October House Farm	2:30:40
1970	High Echelon	John L. Rotz	John W. Jacobs	Ethel D. Jacobs	2:34:00
1969	Arts and Letters	Braulio Baeza	J. Elliott Burch	Rokeby Stables	2:28:80
1968	Stage Door Johnny	Heliodoro Gustines	John M. Gaver Sr.	Greentree Stable	2:27:20
1967	Damascus	Bill Shoemaker	Frank Y. Whiteley, Jr.	Edith W. Bancroft	2:28:80
1966	Amberoid	William Boland	Lucien Laurin	Reginald N. Webster	2:29:60
1965	Hail To All	Johnny Sellers	Eddie Yowell	Zelda Cohen	2:28:40
1964	Quadrangle	Manuel Ycaza	J. Elliott Burch	Rokeby Stables	2:28:40
1963	Chateaugay	Braulio Baeza	James P. Conway	Darby Dan Farm	2:30:20
1962	Jaipur	Bill Shoemaker	Bert Mulholland	George D. Widener Jr.	2:28:80
1961	Sherluck	Braulio Baeza	Harold Young	Jacob Sher	2:29:20
1960	Celtic Ash	Bill Hartack	Thomas J. Barry	Joseph E. O'Connell	2:29:20
1959	Sword Dancer	Bill Shoemaker	J. Elliott Burch	Brookmeade Stable	2:28:40
1958	Cavan	Pete Anderson	Thomas J. Barry	Joseph E. O'Connell	2:30:20
1957	Gallant Man	Bill Shoemaker	John A. Nerud	Ralph Lowe	2:26:60
1956	Needles	David Erb	Hugh L. Fontaine	D & H Stable	2:29:80
1955	Nashua	Eddie Arcaro	Jim Fitzsimmons	Belair Stud	2:29:00

YEAR	WINNER	JOCKEY	TRAINER	OWNER	TIME
1954	High Gun	Eric Guerin	Max Hirsch	King Ranch	2:30:80
1953	Native Dancer	Eric Guerin	Bill Winfrey	Alfred G. Vanderbilt II	2:28:60
1952	One Count	Eddie Arcaro	Oscar White	Sarah F. Jeffords	2:30:20
1951	Counterpoint	David Gorman	Sylvester Veitch	C.V. Whitney	2:29:00
1950	Middleground	William Boland	Max Hirsch	King Ranch	2:28:60
1949	Capot	Ted Atkinson	John M. Gaver Sr.	Greentree Stable	2:30:20
1948	Citation †	Eddie Arcaro	Horace A. Jones	Calumet Farm	2:28:20
1947	Phalanx	Ruperto Donoso	Sylvester Veitch	C.V. Whitney	2:29:40
1946	Assault †	Warren Mehrtens	Max Hirsch	King Ranch	2:30:80
1945	Pavot	Eddie Arcaro	Oscar White	Walter M. Jeffords Sr.	2:30:20
1944	Bounding Home	Gayle Smith	Matt Brady	William Ziegler Jr.	2:32:20
1943	Count Fleet †	Johnny Longden	Don Cameron	Fannie Hertz	2:28:20
1942	Shut Out	Eddie Arcaro	John M. Gaver Sr.	Greentree Stable	2:29:20
1941	Whirlaway †	Eddie Arcaro	Ben A. Jones	CalumetFarm	2:31:00
1940	Bimelech	Fred A. Smith	William J. Hurley	Edward R. Bradley	2:29:60
1939	Johnstown	James Stout	Jim Fitzsimmons	Belair Stud	2:29:60
1938	Pasteurized	James Stout	George M. Odom	Carol Harriman Plunkett	2:29:40
1937	War Admiral †	Charley Kurtsinger	George Conway	Glen Riddle Farm	2:28:60
1936	Granville	James Stout	Jim Fitzsimmons	Belair Stud	2:30:00
1935	Omaha †	Willie Saunders	Jim Fitzsimmons	Belair Stud	2:30:60
1934	Peace Chance	Wayne D. Wright	Pete Coyne	Joseph E. Widener	2:29:20
1933	Hurryoff	Mack Garner	Henry McDaniel	Joseph E. Widener	2:32:60
1932	Faireno	Tommy Malley	Jim Fitzsimmons	Belair Stud	2:32:80
1931	Twenty Grand	Charley Kurtsinger	James G. Rowe Jr.	Greentree Stable	2:29:60
1930	Gallant Fox †	Earl Sande	Jim Fitzsimmons	Belair Stud	2:31:60
1929	Blue Larkspur	Mack Garner	Herbert J. Thompson	Edward R. Bradley	2:32:80
1928	Vito	Clarence Kummer	Max Hirsch	Alfred H. Cosden	2:33:20
1927	Chance Shot	Earl Sande	Pete Coyne	Joseph E. Widener	2:32:40
1926	Crusader	Albert Johnson	George Conway	Glen Riddle Farm	2:32:20

Year	Winner	Jockey	Trainer	Owner	Time
1925	American Flag	Albert Johnson	Gwyn R. Tompkins	Glen Riddle Farm	2:16:80
1924	Mad Play	Earl Sande	Sam Hildreth	Rancocas Stable	2:18:80
1923	Zev	Earl Sande	Sam Hildreth	Rancocas Stable	2:19:00
1922	Pillory	C.H. Miller	Thomas J. Healey	Richard T. Wilson Jr.	2:18:80
1921	Grey Lag	Earl Sande	Sam Hildreth	Rancocas Stable	2:16:80
1920	Man o' War	Clarence Kummer	Louis Feustel	Glen Riddle Farm	2:14:20
1919	Sir Barton †	Johnny Loftus	H. Guy Bedwell	J.K.L. Ross	2:17:40
1918	Johren	Frank Robinson	Albert Simons	Harry P. Whitney	2:20:40
1917	Hourless	James H. Butwell	Sam Hildreth	August Belmont Jr.	2:17:80
1916	Friar Rock	Everett Haynes	Sam Hildreth	August Belmont Jr.	2:22:00
1915	The Finn	George Byrne	Edward W. Heffner	Henry C. Hallenbeck	2:18:40
1914	Luke McLuke	Merritt Buxton	John F. Schorr	John W. Schorr	2:20:00
1913	Prince Eugene	Roscoe Troxler	James G. Rowe Sr.	Harry P. Whitney	2:18:00
1912			NO RACE		
1911					
1910	Sweep	James H. Butwell	James G. Rowe Sr.	James R. Keene	2:22:00
1909	Joe Madden	Eddie Dugan	Sam Hildreth	Sam Hildreth	2:21:60
1908	Colin	Joe Notter	James G. Rowe Sr.	James R. Keene	N/A
1907	Peter Pan	George Mountain	James G. Rowe Sr.	James R. Keene	N/A
1906	Burgomaster	Lucien Lyne	John W. Rogers	Harry P. Whitney	2:20:00
1905	Tanya ‡	Gene Hildebrand	John W. Rogers	Harry P. Whitney	2:08:00
1904	Delhi	George M. Odom	James G. Rowe Sr.	James R. Keene	2:06:60
1903	Africander	John Bullman	Richard O. Miller	Hampton Stable	2:21:75
1902	Masterman	John Bullman	John J. Hyland	August Belmont Jr.	2:22:60
1901	Commando	Henry Spencer	James G. Rowe Sr.	James R. Keene	2:21:00
1900	Ildrim	Nash Turner	H. Eugene Leigh	H. Eugene Leigh	2:21:25
1899	Jean Bereaud	Richard Clawson	Sam Hildreth	Sydney Paget	2:23:00
1898	Bowling Brook	Fred Littlefield	R. Wyndham Walden	A.H. & D.H. Morris	2:32:00
1897	Scottish Chieftain	Joe Scherrer	Matt Byrnes	Marcus Daly	2:23:25

YEAR	WINNER	JOCKEY	TRAINER	OWNER	TIME
1896	Hastings	Henry Griffin	John J. Hyland	Blemton Stable	2:24:50
1895	Belmar	Fred Taral	Edward Feakes	Preakness Stables	2:11:50
1894	Henry of Navarre	Willie Simms	Byron McClelland	Byron McClelland	1:56:50
1893	Commanche	Willie Simms	Gus Hannon	Empire Stable	1:53:25
1892	Patron	William Hayward	Lewis Stuart	Lewis Stuart	2:17:00
1891	Foxford	Edward R. Garrison	M. Donavan	C.E. Rand	2:08:75
1890	Burlington	Pike Barnes	Albert Cooper	Hough Bros.	2:07:75
1889	Eric	William Hayward	John Huggins	A.J. Cassatt	2:47:25
1888	Sir Dixon	Jim McLaughlin	Frank McCabe	Dwyer Bros. Stable	2:40:25
1887	Hanover	Jim McLaughlin	Frank McCabe	Dwyer Bros. Stable	2:43:50
1886	Inspector B	Jim McLaughlin	Frank McCabe	Dwyer Bros. Stable	2:41:00
1885	Tyrant	Paul Duffy	C. Claypool	James B.A. Haggin	2:43:00
1884	Panique	Jim McLaughlin	James G. Rowe Sr.	Dwyer Bros. Stable	2:42:00
1883	George Kinney	Jim McLaughlin	James G. Rowe Sr.	Dwyer Bros. Stable	2:42:50
1882	Forester	Jim McLaughlin	Lewis Stuart	Appleby & Johnson	2:43:00
1881	Saunterer	Tom Costello	R. Wyndham Walden	George L. Lorillard	2:47:00
1880	Grenada	W. Hughes	R. Wyndham Walden	George L. Lorillard	2:47:00
1879	Spendthrift	George Evans	Thomas Puryear	James R. Keene	2:47:75
1878	Duke of Magenta	W. Hughes	R. Wyndham Walden	George L. Lorillard	2:43:50
1877	Cloverbrook	C. Holloway	Jeter Walden	E.A. Clabaugh	2:46:00
1876	Algerine	Billy Donohue	Thomas W. Doswell	Doswell & Co.	2:40:50
1875	Calvin	Bobby Swim	Ansel Williamson	Hal P. McGrath	2:42:25
1874	Saxon	George Barbee	W. Prior	Pierre Lorillard IV	2:39:50
1873	Springbok	James G. Rowe Sr.	David McDaniel	David McDaniel	3:01:75
1872	Joe Daniels	James G. Rowe Sr.	David McDaniel	David McDaniel	2:58:25
1871	Harry Bassett	Walter Miller	David McDaniel	David McDaniel	2:56:00
1870	Kingfisher	Edward D. Brown	Rollie Colston	Daniel Swigert	2:59:50
1869	Fenian	C. Miller	Jacob Pincus	August Belmont	3:04:25
1868	General Duke	Bobby Swim	A. Thompson	McConnell & Co.	3:02:00
1867	Ruthless ‡	Gilbert Patrick	A. Jack Minor	Francis Morris	3:05:00

‡ Denotes a filly

† Denotes a Triple Crown winner

WINNERS OF THE JOCKEY CLUB GOLD CUP

YEAR	WINNER	AGE	JOCKEY	TRAINER	OWNER	TIME
2012	Flat Out	6	Joel Rosario	William I. Mott	Preston Stables	2:01:44
2011	Flat Out	5	Alex Solis	Scooter Dickey	Preston Stables	2:03:17
2010	Haynesfield	4	Ramon Dominguez	Steve Asmussen	Turtle Bird Stable	2:02:48
2009	Summer Bird	3	Kent J. Desormeaux	Tim A. Ice	Jayaraman/Kalarikkal/Vilasini	2:02:51
2008	Curlin	4	Robby Albarado	Steve Asmussen	Stonestreet Stables et al.	2:01:93
2007	Curlin	3	Robby Albarado	Steve Asmussen	Stonestreet Stables et al.	2:01:20
2006	Bernardini	3	Javier Castellano	Thomas Albertrani	Darley Stable	2:01:02
2005	Borrego	4	Garrett Gomez	C. Beau Greely	Kelly, Scott, Ralls, Foster	2:02:86
2004	Funny Cide	4	Jose Santos	Barclay Tagg	Sackatoga Stable	2:02:44
2003	Mineshaft	4	Robby Albarado	Neil J. Howard	Farish, Elkins, Webber	2:00:25
2002	Evening Attire	4	Shaun Bridgmohan	Patrick J. Kelly	Grant, Grant, Kelly	1:59:58
2001	Aptitude	4	Jerry Bailey	Robert J. Frankel	Juddmonte Farm	2:01:49
2000	Albert the Great	3	Jorge Chavez	Nick Zito	Tracy Farmer	1:59:24
1999	River Keen	7	Chris Antley	Bob Baffert	Hugo Reynolds	2:01:40
1998	Wagon Limit	4	Robbie Davis	H. Allen Jerkens	Joseph V. Shields, Jr.	2:00:62
1997	Skip Away	4	Jerry Bailey	Hubert Hine	Carolyn Hine	1:58:89
1996	Skip Away	3	Shane Sellers	Hubert Hine	Carolyn Hine	2:00:70
1995	Cigar	5	Jerry Bailey	William I. Mott	Allen Paulson	2:01:29
1994	Colonial Affair	4	Jose Santos	Flint S. Schulhofer	Centennial Farms	2:02:19
1993	Miner's Mark	3	Chris McCarron	C.R. McGaughey III	Ogden Phipps	2:02:79
1992	Pleasant Tap	5	Gary Stevens	Christopher Speckert	Buckland Farm	1:58:95
1991	Festin	5	Ed Delahoussaye	Ron McAnally	Kinerk Burton	2:00:69
1990	Flying Continental	4	Corey Black	Jay M. Robbins	Jack Kent Cooke	2:00:60
1989	Easy Goer	3	Pat Day	C.R. McGaughey III	Ogden Phipps	2:29:20
1988	Waquoit	5	Jose Santos	Guido Federico	Joseph Federico	2:27:60
1987	Creme Fraiche	5	Laffit Pincay, Jr.	Woody Stephens	Brushwood Stable	2:30:80
1986	Creme Fraiche	4	Randy Romero	Woody Stephens	Brushwood Stable	2:28:00
1985	Vanlandingham	4	Pat Day	C.R. McGaughey III	Loblolly Stable	2:27:00
1984	Slew o' Gold	4	Angel Cordero, Jr.	John O. Hertler	Equusequity Stable	2:28:80
1983	Slew o' Gold	3	Angel Cordero, Jr.	Sidney Watters, Jr.	Equusequity Stable	2:26:20
1982	Lemhi Gold	4	Chris McCarron	Laz Barrera	Aaron U. Jones	2:31:20

YEAR	WINNER	AGE	JOCKEY	TRAINER	OWNER	TIME
1981	John Henry	6	Bill Shoemaker	Victor J. Nickerson	Dotsam Stable	2:28:40
1980	Temperence Hill	3	Eddie Maple	Joseph B. Cantey	Loblolly Stable	2:30:20
1979	Affirmed	4	Laffit Pincay Jr.	Laz Barrera	Harbor View Farm	2:27:40
1978	Exceller	5	Bill Shoemaker	Charles Whittingham	Nelson Bunker Hunt	2:27:20
1977	On The Sly	4	Gregg McCarron	Milton W. Gross	Balmak Stable	2:28:20
1976	Great Contractor	3	Pat Day	Roger Laurin	Howard P. Wilson	2:28:80
1975	Group Plan	5	Jorge Velasquez	H. Allen Jerkens	Hobeau Farm	3:23:20
1974	Forego	4	Heliodoro Gustines	Sherrill W. Ward	Lazy F Ranch	3:21:20
1973	Prove Out	4	Jorge Velasquez	H. Allen Jerkens	Hobeau Farm	3:20:00
1972	Autobiography	4	Angel Cordero Jr.	Pancho Martin	Sigmund Sommer	3:21:40
1971	Shuvee	5	Jorge Velasquez	Willard C. Freeman	Anne Minor Stone	3:20:40
1970	Shuvee	4	Ron Turcotte	Willard C. Freeman	Anne Minor Stone	3:21:60
1969	Arts and Letters	3	Braulio Baeza	J. Elliott Burch	Rokeby Stables	3:22:40
1968	Quicken Tree	5	William Hartack	Clyde Turk	L.R. Rowan/W. Whitney	3:22:80
1967	Damascus	3	Bill Shoemaker	Frank Y. Whiteley, Jr.	Edith W. Bancroft	3:20:20
1966	Buckpasser	3	Braulio Baeza	Edward A. Neloy	Ogden Phipps	3:26:20
1965	Roman Brother	4	Braulio Baeza	Burley Parke	Harbor View Farm	3:22:60
1964	Kelso	7	Ismael Valenzuela	Carl Hanford	Bohemia Stable	3:19:20
1963	Kelso	6	Ismael Valenzuela	Carl Hanford	Bohemia Stable	3:22:00
1962	Kelso	5	Ismael Valenzuela	Carl Hanford	Bohemia Stable	3:19:80
1961	Kelso	4	Eddie Arcaro	Carl Hanford	Bohemia Stable	3:25:80
1960	Kelso	3	Eddie Arcaro	Carl Hanford	Bohemia Stable	3:19:40
1959	Sword Dancer	3	Eddie Arcaro	J. Elliott Burch	Brookmeade Stable	3:22:20
1958	Inside Tract	4	Conn McCreary	John J. Weipert Jr.	D & M Stable	3:23:40
1957	Gallant Man	3	Bill Shoemaker	John A. Nerud	Ralph Lowe	3:23:00
1956	Nashua	4	Eddie Arcaro	Jim Fitzsimmons	Leslie Combs II	3:20:40
1955	Nashua	3	Eddie Arcaro	Jim Fitzsimmons	Belair Stud	3:24:80
1954	High Gun	3	Eddie Arcaro	Max Hirsch	King Ranch	3:25:80
1953	Level Lea	3	William Boland	Not found	John Shaffer Phipps	3:27:00
1952	One Count	3	Dave Gorman	Oscar White	Mrs. Walter M. Jeffords	3:24:20
1951	Counterpoint	3	Dave Gorman	Sylvester Veitch	C.V. Whitney	3:21:60

Year	Winner	Age	Jockey	Trainer	Owner	Time
1950	Hill Prince	3	Dave Gorman	Casey Hayes	Christopher Chenery	3:22:40
1949	Ponder	3	Eddie Arcaro	Ben A. Jones	Calumet Farm	3:22:80
1948	Citation	3	Eddie Arcaro	Ben A. Jones	Calumet Farm	3:21:60
1947	Phalanx	3	Ruperto Donoso	Sylvester Veitch	C.V. Whitney	3:21:60
1946	Pavot	4	Eddie Arcaro	Oscar White	Walter M. Jeffords Sr.	3:22:60
1945	Pot o'Luck	3	Douglas Dodson	Ben A. Jones	Calumet Farm	3:27:40
1944	Bolingbroke	7	Robert Permane	Jim Fitzsimmons	Townsend B. Martin	3:27:20
1943	Princequillo	3	Conn McCreary	Horatio Luro	Boone Hall Stable	3:23:80
1942	Whirlaway	4	George Woolf	Ben A. Jones	Calumet Farm	3:21:60
1941	Market Wise	3	Basil James	George W. Carroll	Louis Tufano	3:20:80
1940	Fenelon	3	James Stout	James E. Fitzsimmons	Belair Stud	3:24:40
1939	Cravat	4	Basil James	Walter Burrows	Townsend B. Martin	3:23:00
1938	War Admiral	4	Wayne D. Wright	George Conway	Glen Riddle Farm	3:24:80
1937	Firethorn	5	Harry Richards	Preston M. Burch	Walter M. Jeffords Sr.	3:26:00
1936	Count Arthur	4	James Stout	Frank Hackett	Fanny Hertz	3:24:40
1935	Firethorn	3	Eddie Arcaro	Preston M. Burch	Walter M. Jeffords Sr.	3:24:20
1934	Dark Secret	5	Charles Kurtsinger	Jim Fitzsimmons	Wheatley Stable	3:24:60
1933	Dark Secret	4	Hank Mills	Jim Fitzsimmons	Wheatley Stable	3:25:20
1932	Gusto	3	Buddy Hanford	Max Hirsch	Morton L. Schwartz	3:25:20
1931	Twenty Grand	3	Charles Kurtsinger	James G. Rowe, Jr.	Greentree Stable	3:23:40
1930	Gallant Fox	3	Earl Sande	Jim Fitzsimmons	Belair Stud	3:24:40
1929	Diavolo	4	John Maiben	Jim Fitzsimmons	Wheatley Stable	3:24:00
1928	Reigh Count	3	Chick Lang	Bert S. Michell	Fanny Hertz	3:23:00
1927	Chance Play	4	Earl Sande	John I. Smith	Log Cabin Stable	3:23:00
1926	Crusader	3	Albert Johnson	George Conway	Glen Riddle Farm	3:26:00
1925	Altawood	3	John Maiben	G. Hamilton Keene	Glen Riddle Farm	3:26:00
1924	My Play	5	Andy Schuttinger	Roy Waldron	Lexington Stable	3:25:60
1923	Homestretch	3	Chick Lang	Ernest Sletas	H. Alterman	3:24:20
1922	Mad Hatter	6	Earl Sande	Sam Hildreth	Rancocas Stable	3:22:60
1921	Mad Hatter	5	Earl Sande	Sam Hildreth	Rancocas Stable	3:22:40
1920	Man o' War	3	Clarence Kummer	Louis Feustel	Glen Riddle Farm	2:28:80
1919	Purchase	3	Clarence Kummer	Sam Hildreth	Glen Riddle Farm	2:28:80

Appendix E

WINNERS OF THE
METROPOLITAN HANDICAP

Year	Winner	Age	Jockey	Trainer	Owner	Time
2012	Shackleford	4	John Velazquez	Dale Romans	Michael Lauffer & W.D. Cubbedge	1:33:30
2011	Tizway	6	Rajiv Maragh	H. James Bond	William Clifton,Jr.	1:32:90
2010	Quality Road	4	John Velazquez	Todd Pletcher	Edward P. Evans	1:33:11
2009	Bribon	6	Alan Garcia	Rob Ribaudo	Marc Keller	1:34:15
2008	Divine Park	4	Alan Garcia	Kiaran McLaughlin	James J. Barry	1:36:91
2007	Corinthian	4	Kent Desormeaux	James A. Jerkens	Centennial Farms	1:34:77
2006	Silver Train	4	Edgar Prado	Richard E. Dutrow Jr.	Buckram Oak Farm	1:34:27
2005	Ghostzapper	5	Javier Castellano	Robert J. Frankel	Stronach Stables	1:33:20
2004	Pico Central	5	Alex Solis	Paulo Lobo	Gary A. Tanaka	1:35:40
2003	Aldebaran	5	Jerry D. Bailey	Robert J. Frankel	Flaxman Holdings	1:34:00
2002	Swept Overboard	5	Jorge F. Chavez	Craig Dollase	J. Paul Reddam	1:33:20
2001	Exciting Story	4	Patrick Husbands	Mark E. Casse	Harry T. Mangurian,Jr.	1:37:00
2000	Yankee Victor	4	Heberto Castillo,Jr.	Carlos Morales	Moreton Binn	1:34:60
1999	Sir Bear	6	John Velazquez	Ralph Ziade	Barbara Smollin	1:34:40
1998	Wild Rush	4	Jerry D. Bailey	Richard Mandella	Stronach Stables	1:33:40
1997	Langfuhr	5	Jorge F. Chavez	Mike Keogh	Gus Schickedanz	1:33:00
1996	Honour and Glory	3	John Velazquez	D. Wayne Lukas	Michael Tabor	1:32:80
1995	You And I	4	Jorge F. Chavez	Robert J. Frankel	Edmund A. Gann	1:34:60
1994	Holy Bull	3	Mike E. Smith	Warren A. Croll Jr.	Warren A. Croll Jr.	1:33:80
1993	Ibero	6	Laffit Pincay Jr.	Ron McAnally	Frank E. Whitham	1:34:20
1992	Dixie Brass	3	Julio Pezua	Dennis J. Brida	Michael Watral	1:33:60
1991	In Excess	4	Pat Valenzuela	Bruce L. Jackson	Jack J. Munari	1:35:40
1990	Criminal Type	5	Jose A. Santos	D. Wayne Lukas	Calumet Farm	1:34:40
1989	Proper Reality	4	Jerry D. Bailey	Robert E. Holthus	Mrs. James A. Winn	1:34:00
1988	Gulch	4	Jose A. Santos	D. Wayne Lukas	Peter M. Brant	1:34:60
1987	Gulch	3	Pat Day	Leroy Jolley	Peter M. Brant	1:34:80
1986	Garthorn	6	Rafael Meza	Robert J. Frankel	Jerome S. Moss	1:33:60
1985	Forzando	4	Don MacBeth	John Sullivan	S.C. Chillingworth	1:34:40
1984	Fit to Fight	5	Jerry D. Bailey	MacKenzie Miller	Rokeby Stable	1:34:00

YEAR	WINNER	AGE	JOCKEY	TRAINER	OWNER	TIME
1983	Star Choice	4	Jorge Velasquez	John M. Veitch	Frances A. Genter	1:33:80
1982	Conquistador Cielo	3	Eddie Maple	Woody Stephens	Henryk de Kwiatkowski	1:33:00
1981	Fappiano	4	Angel Cordero Jr.	Jan H. Nerud	John A. Nerud	1:33:80
1980	Czaravich	4	Laffit Pincay Jr.	William H. Turner Jr.	William L. Reynolds	1:35:80
1979	State Dinner	4	Chris McCarron	William E. Burch	C.V. Whitney	1:34:00
1978	Cox's Ridge	4	Eddie Maple	Joseph B. Cantey	Loblolly Stable	1:34:60
1977	Forego	7	Bill Shoemaker	Frank Y. Whiteley Jr.	Lazy F Ranch	1:34:80
1976	Forego	6	Heliodoro Gustines	Frank Y. Whiteley Jr.	Lazy F Ranch	1:34:80
1975	Gold and Myrrh	4	Walter Blum	William F. Wilmot	William B. Wilmot	1:33:60
1974	Arbees Boy	4	Eddie Maple	George Weckerle Jr.	Orly Stable	1:34:40
1973	Tentam	4	Jorge Velasquez	MacKenzie Miller	Cragwood Stable	1:35:00
1972	Executioner	4	Eddie Belmonte	Eddie Yowell	October House Farm	1:35:40
1971	Tunex	5	John Ruane	H. Allen Jerkens	Hobeau Farm	1:35:80
1970	Nodouble	5	Jorge Tejeira	J. Bert Sonnier	Verna Lea Farm	1:34:60
1969	Arts and Letters	3	Jean Cruguet	J. Elliott Burch	Rokeby Stable	1:34:00
1968	In Reality	4	John L. Rotz	Melvin Calvert	Frances A. Genter	1:35:00
1967	Buckpasser	4	Braulio Baeza	Edward A. Neloy	Ogden Phipps	1:34:60
1966	Bold Lad	4	Braulio Baeza	Edward A. Neloy	Wheatley Stable	1:34:20
1965	Gun Bow	5	Walter Blum	Edward A. Neloy	Gedney Farm	1:34:40
1964	Olden Times	6	Hank Moreno	Mesh Tenney	Rex C. Ellsworth	1:34:40
1963	Cyrano	4	Bobby Ussery	John M. Gaver Sr.	Greentree Stable	1:35:00
1962	Carry Back	4	John L. Rotz	Jack A. Price	Katherine Price	1:33:60
1961	Kelso	4	Eddie Arcaro	Carl Hanford	Bohemia Stable	1:35:60
1960	Bald Eagle	5	Manuel Ycaza	Woody Stephens	Cain Hoy Stable	1:33:60
1959	Sword Dancer	3	Bill Shoemaker	J. Elliott Burch	Brookmeade Stable	1:35:20
1958	Gallant Man	4	Bill Shoemaker	John A. Nerud	Ralph Lowe	1:35:60
1957	Traffic Judge	5	Eddie Arcaro	James W. Maloney	Louis P. Doherty	1:36:00
1956	Midafternoon	4	William Boland	Thomas M. Waller	Mrs. Edward E. Robbins	1:35:00
1955	High Gun	4	Anthony DeSpirito	Max Hirsch	King Ranch	1:35:60

Year	Winner	Age	Jockey	Trainer	Owner	Time
1954	Native Dancer	4	Eric Guerin	William C. Winfrey	Alfred G. Vanderbilt II	1:35:20
1953	Tom Fool	4	Ted Atkinson	John M. Gaver Sr.	Greentree Stable	1:35:80
1952	Mameluke	4	Gerald Porch	Sylvester Veitch	C.V. Whitney	1:36:40
1951	Casemate	4	Dave Gorman	Robert Dotter	James Cox Brady Jr.	1:35:40
1950	Greek Ship	3	Hedley Woodhouse	Preston M. Burch	Brookmeade Stable	1:36:60
1949	Loser Weeper	4	Hedley Woodhouse	William C. Winfrey	Alfred G. Vanderbilt II	1:36:40
1948	Stymie	7	Conn McCreary	Hirsch Jacobs	Ethel D. Jacobs	1:36:80
1947	Stymie	6	Basil James	Hirsch Jacobs	Ethel D. Jacobs	1:37:40
1946	Gallorette	4	Job Dean Jessop	Edward A. Christmas	William L. Brann	1:37:00
1945	Devil Diver	6	Ted Atkinson	John M. Gaver Sr.	Greentree Stable	1:36:40
1944	Devil Diver	5	Ted Atkinson	John M. Gaver Sr.	Greentree Stable	1:35:80
1943	Devil Diver	4	George Woolf	John M. Gaver Sr.	Greentree Stable	1:36:60
1942	Attention	4	Don Meade	Max Hirsch	Mrs. Parker Corning	1:36:40
1941	Eight Thirty	5	Harry Richards	Bert Mulholland	George D. Widener Jr.	1:37:20
1940	Third Degree	4	Eddie Arcaro	John M. Gaver Sr.	Greentree Stable	1:35:40
1939	Knickerbocker	3	Fred A. Smith	Pete Coyne	Joseph E. Widener	1:37:20
1938	Danger Point	4	Eddie Arcaro	Eddie Hayward	James D. Norris	1:38:00
1937	Snark	4	Johnny Longden	James Fitzsimmons	Wheatley Stable	1:37:80
1936	Good Harvest	4	Sam Remick	Bud Stotler	Alfred G. Vanderbilt II	1:36:40
1935	King Saxon	4	Calvin Rainey	C.H. Knebelkamp	C.H. Knebelkamp	1:38:20
1934	Mr. Khayyam	4	Robert Jones	Matthew P. Brady	Catawba Farm	1:37:00
1933	Equipoise	5	Raymond Workman	Thomas J. Healey	C.V. Whitney	1:37:40
1932	Equipoise	4	Raymond Workman	Thomas J. Healey	C.V. Whitney	1:37:00
1931	Questionnaire	4	Raymond Workman	Andy Schuttinger	James Butler	1:38:60
1930	Jack High	4	Linus McAtee	A. Jack Joyner	George D. Widener Jr.	1:35:00
1929	Petee-Wrack	4	Steve O'Donnell	Willie Booth	John R. Macomber	1:40:00
1928	Nimba	4	Harold Thurber	George M. Odom	Marshall Field III	1:40:00
1927	Black Maria	4	Frank Coltiletti	William H. Karrick	William R. Coe	1:37:40
1926	Sarazen	5	Fred Weiner	Max Hirsch	Fair Stable	1:38:00
1925	Sting	4	Bennie Breuning	Jimmy Johnson	James Butler	1:37:00

Year	Winner	Age	Jockey	Trainer	Owner	Time
1924	Laurano	3	Harold Thurber	Johnny Loftus	Oak Ridge Stable	1:38:20
1923	Grey Lag	5	Earl Sande	Sam Hildreth	Rancocas Stable	1:38:00
1922	Mad Hatter	6	Earl Sande	Sam Hildreth	Rancocas Stable	1:36:60
1921	Mad Hatter	5	Earl Sande	Sam Hildreth	Rancocas Stable	1:37:40
1920	Wildair	3	Eddie Ambrose	James G. Rowe Sr.	Harry Payne Whitney	1:38:80
1919	Lanius	3	Johnny Loftus	A. Jack Joyner	George D. Widener Jr.	1:42:40
1918	Trompe La Mort	3	Linus McAtee	Thomas Welch	Joseph E. Widener	1:38:40
1917	Ormesdale	4	John McTaggart	Thomas J. Healey	Richard T. Wilson Jr.	1:39:20
1916	The Finn	4	Andy Schuttinger	Edward W. Heffner	Henry C. Hallenbeck	1:38:00
1915	Stromboli	4	Clarence Turner	Sam Hildreth	August Belmont Jr.	1:39:80
1914	Buskin	4	Charles Fairbrother	John Whalen	John Whalen	1:37:80
1913	Whisk Broom II	6	Joe Notter	James G. Rowe Sr.	Harry Payne Whitney	1:39:00
1912				*NO RACE*		0:00:00
1911						0:00:00
1910	Fashion Plate	4	Matthew McGee	William H. Karrick	Oneck Stable	1:37:80
1909	King James	4	Guy Burns	John E. Madden	Sam Hildreth	1:40:00
1908	Jack Atkin	4	Carroll H. Shilling	Herman R. Brandt	Barney Schreiber	1:38:60
1907	Glorifier	5	Charles Garner	James H. McCormick	James H. McCormick	1:40:80
1906	Grapple	4	Charles Garner	Enoch Wishard	John A. Drake	1:39:00
1905	Race King (DH)	4	L. Smith	Jim McLaughlin	O.L. Richard	1:41:60
1905	Sysonby (DH)	3	Willie Shaw	James G. Rowe Sr.	James R. Keene	1:41:60
1904	Irish Lad	4	Willie Shaw	John E. Madden	Herman B. Duryea	1:40:00
1903	Gunfire	4	Tommy Burns	John W. Rogers	William C. Whitney	1:38:00
1902	Arsenal	3	J. Daly	Julius Bauer	Arthur L. Featherstone	1:42:50
1901	Banastar	6	George M. Odom	Charles F. Hill	Charles H. Mackay	1:42:00
1900	Ethelbert	4	Danny Maher	A. Jack Joyner	Perry Belmont	1:41:00
1899	Filigrane	4	Richard Clawson	R. Wyndham Walden	A.H. Morris & D.H. Morris	1:39:25
1898	Bowling Brook	3	Pete Clay	R. Wyndham Walden	A.H. Morris & D.H. Morris	1:44:00
1897	Voter	3	John Lamley	William Lakeland	James R. Keene	1:40:00

APPENDIX E

YEAR	WINNER	AGE	JOCKEY	TRAINER	OWNER	TIME
1896	Counter Tenor	4	Anthony Hamilton	William Lakeland	Jacob Ruppert Jr.	1:53:00
1895			NO RACE			0:00:00
1894	Ramapo	4	Fred Taral	John J. Hyland	Gideon & Daly	1:52:50
1893	Charade	4	Samuel Doggett	Not Found	W.R. Jones	1:52:25
1892	Pessara	4	Fred Taral	John Campbell	Walcott & Campbell	1:54:00
1891	Tristan	3	George Taylor	Not Found	L. Stuart & Co.	1:51:50

150

Appendix G

WINNERS OF THE
MARLBORO CUP

Year	Winner	Age	Jockey	Trainer	Owner	Time
1973	Secretariat	3	Ron Turcotte	Lucien Laurin	Meadow Stable	1:45:40
1974	Big Spruce	5	Michael Hole	Victor J. Nickerson	Elmendorf Farm	1:46:60
1975	Wajima	3	Braulio Baeza	Stephen A. DiMauro	East-West Stable	2:00:00
1976	Forego	6	Bill Shoemaker	Frank Y. Whiteley Jr.	Lazy F Ranch	2:00:00
1977	Proud Birdie	4	Jacinto Vasquez	James W. Maloney	Marablue Farm	2:00:80
1978	Seattle Slew	4	Angel Cordero Jr.	Douglas R. Peterson	Karen & Mickey Taylor	1:45:80
1979	Spectacular Bid	3	Bill Shoemaker	Bud Delp	Hawksworth Farm	1:46:60
1980	Winter's Tale	4	Jeffrey Fell	MacKenzie Miller	Rokeby Stables	1:47:00
1981	Noble Nashua	3	Ruben Hernandez	Jose A. Martin	Flying Zee Stable	2:00:60
1982	Lemhi Gold	4	Jacinto Vasquez	Laz Barrera	Aaron U. Jones	2:01:00
1983	Highland Blade	4	Jacinto Vasquez	David A. Whiteley	Pen-Y-Bryn Farm	2:01:20
1984	Slew o' Gold	4	Angel Cordero Jr.	John O. Hertler	Equusequity Stable	2:02:40
1985	Chief's Crown	3	Don MacBeth	Roger Laurin	Star Crown Stable	2:01:20
1986	Turkoman	4	Gary Stevens	Gary F. Jones	Saron Stable	2:00:00
1987	Java Gold	3	Pat Day	MacKenzie Miller	Rokeby Stables	2:01:00

NOTES

CHAPTER ONE

1. www.encyclopedia.com/topic/horse_racing.aspx.
2. http://daytoninmanhattan.blogspot.com/2011/10/lost-1859-leonard-jerome-mansion.html.
3. *New York Times*, December 30, 1894.
4. *New York Daily Tribune*, September 26, 1866.

CHAPTER THREE

5. *New York Times*, June 6, 1867.

CHAPTER FOUR

6. Richard Stone Reeves and Edward L. Bowen, *Belmont Park: A Century of Champions* (Lexington, KY: Eclipse Press, 2005), 11.

CHAPTER FIVE

7. *Life* magazine, July 21, 1963.
8. *New York Tribune*, May 5, 1905.

9. *New York Times*, June 1905.

10. Ibid.

11. Reeves and Bowen, *Belmont Park*.

CHAPTER SIX

12. http://www.nationalsteeplechase.com/chasing/history.

13. Kent Hollingsworth, *The Great Ones* (Lexington, KY: Bloodhorse, 1970).

14. *New York Times*, November 5, 1909.

CHAPTER SEVEN

15. horseracing.about.com/od/famoushorses/l/blmanwar.htm.

CHAPTER EIGHT

16. *New York Times*, August 22, 1920.

CHAPTER NINE

17. Bryan Field, "Gallant Fox Beats Whichone 4 Lengths in $81,340 Belmont," *New York Times*, June 8, 1930.

18. *National Turf Digest*, September 1930, 917.

19. *The Blood Horse*, June 15, 1935.

CHAPTER TEN

20. *New York Times*, June 8, 1941.

21. Ibid., 1940.

22. Ibid., June 2, 1944.

Chapter Eleven

23. http://www.spiletta.com/UTHOF/nativedancer.html
24. *Sports Illustrated*, May 2, 1955.
25. http://sportsillustrated.cnn.com/vault/article/magazine/MAG1002384.
26. http://www.drf.com/news/carl-hanford-dies-trained-kelso.
27. Reeves and Bowen, *Belmont Park*.
28. *Baltimore Sun*, "Canonero Came Close To Triple Crowning Glory," September 26, 1991.

Chapter Twelve

29. *New York Times*, June 10, 1973.
30. *Sports Illustrated*, September 2, 1974.
31. http://www.spiletta.com/UTHOF/ruffian.html.
32. http://www.spiletta.com/UTHOF/ruffian.html.

Chapter Thirteen

33. *New York Times*, October 8, 1989

Chapter Fifteen

34. http://www.sptimes.com/2003/06/08/Sports/Empire_strikes_back_a.shtml.

INDEX

ABOUT THE AUTHOR

K imberly Gatto is a professional writer specializing in equestrian and sports books. Her published works to date include six horse-related titles and seven athlete biographies. Kim's work has been included in various publications, including the *Blood Horse*, the *Chronicle of the Horse*, the *Equine Journal* and *Chicken Soup for the Horse Lover's Soul*. Other History Press books by Gatto include *Churchill Downs: America's Most Historic Racetrack*, *Saratoga Race Course: The August Place to Be* and *Belair Stud: Cradle of Maryland Horse Racing*. Gatto is an honors graduate of Boston Latin School and Wheaton College. A lifelong rider and horsewoman, she is the proud owner of a lovely off-the-track Thoroughbred and an adorable Welsh pony.